TO THE
CHILDREN
OF
ISRAEL

SPEAK
TO THE
CHILDREN
OF
ISRAEL

Edited by
RABBI SAMUEL M. SILVER
and
RABBI MORTON M. APPLEBAUM

KTAV PUBLISHING HOUSE, INC.

1976

Library of Congress Cataloging in Publication Data

Main entry under title:

Speak to the children of Israel.

SUMMARY: Brief sermons dealing with various aspects of the human condition, stressing the Jewish principles for living.
1. Homiletical illustrations, Jewish. 2. Children's sermons, Jewish. 3. Sermons, American—Jewish authors. 4. Sermons, Jewish — United States. [1. Sermons. 2. Jewish religious education. 3. Conduct of life] I. Silver, Samuel M. II. Applebaum, Morton M.
BM733.S67   296.7'4   76-39947

ISBN 0-87068-495-7

CONTENTS

We dedicate this book to
ELEANOR and ELAINE
Who have filled our lives
with "E's."

Foreword

Of the telling of stories there is no end.

But *what* is the end of a story with a religious setting? In other words, what do the stories hope to achieve?

Using homiletical license, we suggest that one way of answering that question is through a word-play. The aim of a story is to defy, to edify and to deify.

To *defy* the inroads of hopelessness and faithlessness, a sermon should make the listener aware of the fact that he has it in himself to combat these foes. A person once asked who are the "enemies" referred to in Psalm 23. The answer is that the "enemies" are not people but defeatist states of mind. A pulpit presentation is meant to defy the effects of despair and melancholy.

To *edify*. The dull sermon defeats its purpose. Anecdotes, illustrations, the examples of great men and women vivify and illuminate the points made by the preacher. But although the sermon pleads with us to entertain loftier thoughts, it is not entertainment as such; it is engrossment with a purpose.

To *deify*. Ever since the Golden Calf, man has tended to apotheosize parts of nature instead of their Author. In modern times there are men who seek to lift Nothingness upon the altars of human devotion. The sermon should make it clear that the mature person makes God his Sovereign, as that Sovereign has made us little lower than the angels.

We believe that the homilies, talks and messages in this volume fulfill these three purposes. When our previous volume was published, we were delighted with the fine reception given it and we were almost at once importuned to gather together another cluster. We herewith do so, with thanks to the illustrious authors of the stories, and with special thanks to our secretaries, Mrs. Harry Meltzer and Mrs. Milton Weissman, who were of immense aid.

Rabbis Morton M. Applebaum and Samuel M. Silver

* * *

The Mystery of God

Two men, one a university professor, an able physicist, and the other an intelligent and deeply religious farmer, met at a party. In the course of their conversation which had turned to religion, the professor said to the farmer, "But how can you be so sure of the existence of God? And if God is so real to you, perhaps you can explain something about His mystery."

"Well," answered the farmer, "I'm really not as informed about religious matters as I wish I were. But I do very definitely believe in God. As you know I am a farmer and that's what I know most about." And noticing a few slices of watermelon on a table nearby, he directed the attention of the professor to them and continued, "Have you ever observed the watermelon seed? I have. It has the power of drawing from the ground and through itself 200,000 times its weight, and when you can tell me how it takes this material and out of it colors an outside surface beyond the imitation of art, and then forms inside of it a white rind and within again a red heart, thickly inlaid with black seeds, each one of which in turn is capable of drawing through itself 200,000 times its weight—when you can explain to me the mystery of a watermelon, you can ask me to explain the mystery of God."

The professor was impressed and added, "You have

observed well and spoken wisely. But there is one thing you said with which I disagree. You acknowledged knowing your farming but felt inadequate in theology. I must beg to differ with you. Your reasoning about the mystery of God through the mystery of a watermelon is as sound as any I have ever heard. Thank you for sharing it with me.''

Rabbi Morton M. Applebaum

* * *

Thoughts after a Rough Flight

Rough airplane flights are becoming fewer and fewer as radar instruments help aircraft to bypass stormy and turbulent areas. But there was a certain flight I took from Ottawa to Toronto that I shall never forget. I had flown into Ottawa that morning and had to be back in Toronto that night. Though the plane for Toronto was going to make the flight, all passengers were told that the flight would be rough because there was no way of avoiding the turbulence between the two cities. The airline was prepared to take those who preferred to wait for a morning flight back to an Ottawa hotel and assume all the charges. Most of the passengers accepted the offer. But I had to make it back to Toronto, and since the plane was going to take off, I decided to go.

It was a rough ride. The night was pitch dark and

stormy; the visibility left much to be desired. The five of us who risked it wore our seat-belts all the way. The aircraft "upped" and "downed" like a bobber on a swell. None of us knew the captain who was at the controls. I certainly could not be sure whether he had ever flown through such turbulence before. It was possible that it might even be too rough for him. It was possible that he was so exhausted and blear-eyed that he might be having a very difficult time making the runway without a mishap. And yet, believing he was trustworthy, else he would not be in so responsible a position, I tried to relax as best I could between those dives and climbs. Actually, when we began to descend for the runway, I awoke from a brief shut-eye.

I did not feel I did a foolhardy act, dozing off as I had, though pilots have had mishaps occur under similar circumstances, have veered off runways or even ditched their planes. And yet I trusted my life to a man I had never seen, and under most unfavorable circumstances. Hundreds of thousands of air travelers do that very thing daily.

And now when I think about trusting in God—how much should we trust in Him, an overruling invisible Providence guiding His children through all the storms and darkness of life. If I and millions flying entrust our lives to pilots unknown to us whom we have never seen, shall not this faith be matched by at least the same in our God?

Rabbi Morton M. Applebaum

* * *

I Don't Feel Like It!

There is a story about a prominent college football coach who noticed that one of his players was not falling on the football in the way in which he had directed the members of the team to do. "Why don't you fall on the ball the way I have told you to?" he said to the player. And the latter stubbornly replied: "I don't feel like it." "Then," said the coach, "leave the field and turn in your equipment."

The player did so and he was not allowed to finish out that season with the team. He was—with possibly two exceptions—the best man on the team, strong as an ox, heavy, tall, agile, and a very swift runner. That college was not a particularly large school and actually had only a mere handful of players. No one dreamed that the coach would ever dare to weaken the team by laying off such an exceptionally fine player. In fact, that player felt so sure of himself because of his importance to the team that he was taking advantage of the situation.

The very next game was a most important one. The stadium was filled to capacity. Every student and faculty member of the college must have been in the stands, and many of the alumni were there for this important game. And there in the stands also sat the player who had been so important to the team.

Well, the game ended with the team of the small college taking a real shellacking. The coach was booed by some. A delegation of the alumni met with him, and wanted to know why he had been so hard on that important member of the team.

6

"Gentlemen," he said, "years of experience have taught me the necessity of requiring absolute obedience from all of my players. There can be no privileged characters. Furthermore, there are three kinds of people in the world, the "wills," the "can'ts," and the "won'ts": The first accomplish everything; the second fail in everything; the third are just ornery, oppose everything and contribute very little, in anything. This player merely did not feel like doing what he was supposed to do. Disobedience removed his value to us."

The coach did not have to say anymore. What he said also got around the student body. The whole college learned a lesson. And as for those whoever played for him, they never again disobeyed his orders.

Rabbi Morton M. Applebaum

* * *

Shabbat Means Stop

I have a three-year-old son whose friend, a next-door neighbor, is five. Ricky, the neighbor, is Christian. He spends a lot of time with my son, teaching him all kinds of skills and new words, too. Ricky can do things that my boy can't do, but this doesn't make Ricky bossy; it makes him a teacher of his younger friend.

Ricky visits us very often on Friday night when we welcome the Sabbath at the table. His eyes open wide when Mother thanks God for the light of the Shabbat candles. He gazes in such wonder at each of us as we hold up our cups to recite the sweetening words of the Kiddush that we give him a cup to hold, too (with milk, like our little ones have). He has learned the words of the Motzi, the thank-you prayer for bread which we all sing together, preceded by the chant: "Our voices join in song together as our prayer is humbly said."

In fact, Ricky became so enchanted with our Friday night Shabbat welcome, that something amusing happened. Once his mother was visiting our house, and was gaily chatting with my wife. Suddenly Ricky came over to his mother and blurted out, "Mom, why can't *we* have Shabbat!"

A few days later, I said to Ricky, "You can have Shabbat, if you want to have it." He said, "How?"

I said, "All you have to do is what Shabbat wants you to do."

"What does it want me to do?" he asked. At this my own son came closer, too. He doesn't entirely understand what grown-ups like Ricky and I mean, but he catches some of it.

"Well, Ricky, Shabbat is a Hebrew word," I began.

"What does it mean?" he asked.

"It means stop."

"Stop?"

"Yes . . . . stop," I explained. "When you see the candles getting lit, they say to you: stop being a cry-baby. Be bright, like we are. So, Ricky, whenever

8

you want to whine or cry but laugh instead, you're having Shabbat. And what's more important, if you can make other people feel good instead of bad, that's really Shabbat. If you are about to hit another child or hurt him and then you remember the smiling Shabbat candles and you stop yourself, that's Shabbat, too. Understand?"

"Uh, huh," said Ricky.

"That's what Shabbat is for. It says stop doing the things that will hurt people. Stop making others feel bad. Stop being a little boy; start acting like a big one." I looked at Ricky to see whether he grasped the meaning of my explanation.

I wasn't sure. But, then, Shabbat comes every week. It never stops telling us to put a stop to our bad habits. And it never stops urging us to add a "little Shabbat" to every day of the week.

Rabbi Samuel M. Silver

* * *

Beware of the Ghost

It happened in Germany about a hundred and twenty years ago, in a factory which stood on the outskirts of a town. The factory was not a modern one. It did not use steam or electricity. Its work was done entirely by hand.

9

The output of the factory consisted of men's caps, and the workers were teenaged boys. They were Jewish boys. But the proprietor of the factory was not Jewish.

When autumn approached, the boys looked forward to the Jewish High Holy Days. They asked the proprietor to let them off from their work for the two days of their Jewish New Year; and then, for a day, the following week, that they might observe the Day of Atonement. The proprietor found himself perplexed. He had a large backlog of orders, getting ready for the Christmas trade. How could he afford to keep his factory closed for three whole days?

He explained those matters to the boys. Then there occurred to him a happy thought. "Boys," he said, "I want you to observe your holidays. I want you to have those three days off. Why not do this? For a week before your New Year, bring with you every morning, not only your lunches but your suppers as well, and remain at the factory for a few hours every evening. In that way we can make up, in advance, what we lost by omitting work on your holidays."

The boys were satisfied. Every day, for a week prior to the Jewish New Year, they brought their suppers as well as their lunches. They remained at the factory every evening, and worked almost until midnight.

The work was not very hard. It was simple and easily learnt. The one drawback was the monotony. To relieve the monotony, the boys would, while working, talk, joke, laugh, and sing. The proprietor did not object to such diversions, so long as the employees' fingers kept busy at their tasks.

10

Thus, evening after evening, while they worked, the boys entertained one another with stories, anecdotes, and songs. But, as the Jewish New Year drew near, one of them asked a gruesome question. He asked: "Is it not a fact that, on the Jewish New Year and Day of Atonement, the Jewish dead get up from their graves and attend the religious services? Those dead are invisible to human eyes but, if we could see them, we would notice them occupying their former places in the synagogue, wearing their white shrouds, holding their prayer books in their bony hands, intently taking part in the ritual."

In those days and in that part of the world superstitions were rife. People believed anything that sounded weird. That boy's question had a sobering effect. It throttled all laughing and singing. The young fellows then began a line of ghost stories, one more uncanny than the other, stories such as, we say, "make one's hair stand on end." There was no further merriment. There was shuddering; there was trembling. Some of the boys became too scared to look around.

Shortly before midnight the whistle sounded the end of the evening's work. The boys rose from their tables. They blew out the lights. They left for their homes. One of them carried a lantern. But, between the factory and their homes, lay a stretch of open country and a lonely road. After hearing those "spook" stories, the boys, on their way homeward, appeared too frightened to talk and almost too frightened to walk.

Then came the supreme terror! After they had gone a short distance, the boys saw a tall white thing standing

11

in the road! They were almost paralyzed with horror. They started to turn around and run back in the direction from which they had come, all except one of them, the oldest in the group, a youth who had outgrown a few of the neighborhood superstitions. Instead of turning around and running back, that boy ran forward. He ran up to the dreadful white shape. He ran up to it and kicked it.

"Come back, fellows," he shouted, "someone whitewashed that old tree, getting ready for the New Year."

What a sense of relief came over the boys when they saw that the ghastly specter was nothing but a whitewashed tree! From that time onward they no longer believed in ghosts. As the years passed and they grew to manhood, they learnt how often the things of which we are afraid turn out to be "whitewashed trees," utterly harmless.

People again and again stand in dread of things that never happen. They live in dread of windstorms that do little damage, dread of some illness which never comes, dread of mishaps to dear ones who have merely, for one reason or another, been delayed, or dread of someone's hostility when no hostile feelings existed. They even dread people's unfavorable opinion when it turns out afterward that those people had expended never a thought on the worried person.

This is not to deny that some dangers are real. Some things do cause harm. Some things do have to be shunned. Our chief perils lie in our own traits, such as carelessness, laziness, dishonesty, rage, discourtesy, inattentiveness, not to mention such physical matters as overeating, intemperance, or failure to heed the doctor. These are the dangers most likely to befall us. Otherwise, most of what we fear is as imaginary as that which alarmed those boys.

Rabbi Abraham Cronbach

* * *

Black and White

We use the phrase "black on white" when we refer to the printed page. Some printers are experimenting with another type of page, the paper black and the type white. They say that this new method of white on black will be just as clear and more restful to the eyes. These two types of record, black on white and white on black, come to mind when we see how the Scripture describes God's guidance of Israel through the desert as they left Egypt. He guided them with a dark cloud against the bright sky, which was "black on white," and then with a bright fire of cloud against the dark night sky, which was "white on black." There are two ways in which God guides us: through dark things against brightness and through bright things against darkness.

Black on White. The pillar of cloud is a symbol of the tiny storm against the normal, sunny skies of life.

These storms should be watched as Israel watched the pillar of cloud. For example, young people in their teens are often sullen, hidden under a cloud of secrecy. That is normal. Young people are entitled to their private thoughts and secrets, but watch that dark cloud. It is dangerous. This sullen withdrawal, this refusal to discuss things with parents may spread until it is a dark cloud, until it covers the entire heavens of life and becomes complete estrangement between parent and child. Keep your secrets but make up for them by additional intimacies and comradeship with your parents. Watch with great care the dark cloud against the brightness of life.

White on Black. The little bright light is beautifully described by the famous Bishop Brooks of Massachusetts. He speaks of a party exploring the Mammoth Caves of Kentucky. While they were out in the sunlight, they were given lighted candles which they held carelessly, since the skies were bright and the candlelight seemed weak; but when they got into the darkness of the cave, they held on with all their might to "the light they once despised."

In all our teachings in religious school, we try to give you candlelight of faith. You may not appreciate it, but in times of darkness, you will hold onto it with all your strength. It is the light of religion which is the main object of all our instruction, and is the bright pillar of fire against the dark clouds of sorrow.

In the High Holy Day services we often use the phrase "The Book of Life." That book has two kinds of writing, black on white and white on black. We learn by

14

both experiences: the dark little storms of anger and the little candle flame of faith. May they both guide us as Israel was guided through the desert, by pillars of cloud and fire, until we reach the promised land of a happy and useful life.

Rabbi Solomon B. Freehof

* * *

Making and Keeping Friends

Among the books published in the nineteen sixties, was a best-seller entitled *How to Win Friends*. It seems strange that hundreds of thousands of people wanted to buy a book which proposed to tell them how to win friends. Evidently most people discover that winning friends is not as simple as it might seem. In fact, it is an important task which involves human character. One might say that the first part of one of our Scriptural readings involves this very task. Jacob, returning after twenty years, knows that he must make friends with Esau, his brother, since they had parted in anger.

Not Boasting but Modesty. Jacob sends messengers ahead to Esau and instructs them carefully as to what they should say, namely: "Thus saith thy servant Jacob." Now Jacob was no human being's servant. He was, by now, a highly successful man, and yet he preferred the modest speech because he knew that boastfulness destroys friendship and that modesty creates it. If in conversation you always talk of yourself and of your achievements, the person to whom you are boasting is made to feel that he is nobody compared with you, and therefore he will avoid you if he can in the future. Modesty in speech involves a respect for the standing and achievements of others. It is a great help in achieving friendship to fulfill the command of the Book of Proverbs: "Let others praise thee, not thine own mouth."

Not Asking but Giving. After he had spoken so modestly to Esau, he sent Esau some gifts. Not that he meant to buy friendship by giving presents; Esau did not need the flocks and herds that Jacob sent. Jacob meant, by his gift, to symbolize the fact that he wanted Esau's friendship, but not for the purpose of receiving favors. Nothing destroys friendship so much as the constant asking for things. When a man speaks modestly, but after a few modest sentences immediately asks you for something, you have the right to doubt the sincerity of his modest manner. With friendship it is as with happiness. The only way to find happiness is to give it. The only way to find a friend is to be a friend.

Perhaps Dale Carnegie's best-seller should have been given a different title. The real problem is not how to *win* friends, but how to *keep* friends. When we are young, we naturally pick up many friends. But as we get older we sadly realize we are losing scores and scores of them. Some we cannot help losing because we move away into a different region and we just forget each other. But those whom we see we ought never to lose.

16

The people who, like our father Jacob, refrain from childish boasting and maintain a quiet modesty, those who consider their friends not people from whom to get favors but those to whom to do a kindness, such will never be alone; they will always be surrounded by affectionate and trusting friends.

Rabbi Solomon B. Freehof

* * *

Equal in Duty

A citizen has two main duties to his country: to pay his taxes and to cast his vote. There is, however, a difference between the two duties. The amount of taxes we pay varies from citizen to citizen, but each citizen casts only one vote. The taxes reveal our different contributions; the vote represents our equal duty. The same distinction between different contributions and equal duty is found in Scripture. When the Tabernacle was first planned, each man was asked to give according to his means and impulses, ''as his heart prompts him.'' Each one had to give as a contribution to the Tabernacle a half of a silver shekel. We make different contributions to our religion according to our ability; but since ours is a democratic religion, we must find ways in which, also, we can give precisely the same gift, as if we were casting a vote for our faith.

Temple and Worship. Temples are supported by dues. In most temples the dues are graduated in amount according to each member's desire and ability to give. Yet there is one important way in which we are all alike. The duty to be present at service is uniquely democratic. The richest cannot bring more than himself, nor the poorest less. Our presence is our "sacred silver coin," with which gift we are all equal. Each one is a worshipper whose presence is a vote of confidence in God's administration of the world. If we all carried out this equal duty of attendance, the impact of our religion would be grand and powerful in every department of our life.

School and Education. Our young people are not expected to attend services regularly, but they must attend our religious school regularly. They, too, are not equal in their gifts to the school. Some children are brighter than others. Some can concentrate better than others. The slower ones will very likely catch up later; but for the present, their contributions to the school vary "as their mind prompts them." But in one way they are all equal. Each must give his best effort, his honest desire to learn. No one can do more than that. No one should do less.

How many Children of Israel were there in the desert? Moses did not quite know. They needed to be numbered. Therefore, when each one gave the same silver half shekel, these gifts were counted and thus the number was known. Scripture means to say that we are

18

counted by what we give, not by what we take. What we give to God is in a definite sense an equal gift from each. Adults give the gift of their presence at worship. Young people give the gift of their effort at school. Thus does our religion show itself to be a democracy and our temple a sanctuary and tabernacle of God.

Rabbi Solomon B. Freehof

* * *

Only a Few

In Genesis 18 there is a debate between Abraham and God. God said He would destroy the evil city of Sodom if He finds it to be as evil as it was reported to be. Abraham finally persuades God to save the city if there are ten righteous people in it. This does not appear logical. If the city had ten thousand inhabitants and nine thousand, nine hundred and ninety were evil, then surely the city was thoroughly corrupted and should not be saved. The ten righteous might well be rescued, but should a city be saved when it is so saturated with evil? Evidently there is a deep, unexpressed meaning in the text. It implies that ten righteous may outweigh and eventually influence nine thousand, nine hundred and ninety evil people; that truth and goodness have an inner power which enables them to overcome a mountain of evil. We know that historically this has proven to be true. The people of Israel were a small handful of worshipers of the true God in an entire world of idolatry. Yet the truth held by a handful saved mankind from paganism. This, then, must also be true in personal life: "A handful can save the city."

Personal Careers. A school teacher studies carefully each new class at the beginning of the year. How many of these young people will learn to enjoy reading and become cultured? How many will learn the discipline of work and rise in profession or business some day? If thirty years later she thinks back on that year's class and finds that ten out of the entire class attained culture or a worthy career, she will be proud and grateful. It does not take many to make a year's teaching worthwhile.

Public Service. When young people grow up and begin to explore the possibilities of communal service, they are often shocked to discover how few people there are who are willing to do the work of maintaining an organization. Large numbers of people may belong to the organization, a much smaller number attends its meetings or the religious services of the congregation, but only a very small number will take the burden of responsibility or leadership and active work. After their surprise wears off, these young people discover that it never takes more than a few who are strong enough to carry the burden of responsibility. A handful of devoted workers maintain every institution of worth.

The great New England minister, Wendell Philips, was one of the early advocates of liberty for the Negro slaves. Sometimes he must have been discouraged that

20

there were so few people on his side in this great cause, but he always consoled himself by realizing that it does not take many to do great things. It was he who said, "One man on God's side makes a majority." This is the vital meaning in the story of the debate between God and Abraham. It teaches: Do not always look to be sheltered by the majority. If you know the truth, speak it. If you have a worthy task to do, do it. If your conscience is clear, you may well become a majority. Ten righteous people can save the city.

Rabbi Solomon B. Freehof

* * *

The Sacrifice Hit

When the baseball season arrives I see the boys out in the street batting with all their might. And on the sandlots, the arms are getting a workout.

I can never forget my first lesson in team play. Like other boys, I used to play worky-up. With less than enough boys to make two teams, we used to play in rotating positions. You might start in the outfield, work up to third, then second, first, pitcher, catcher and then at bat. And you stayed at bat as long as you were not put out. Once out, you started at the bottom of the ladder again.

Now, in such a game you did not play for score.

21

There really was no score because there were no sides, so you did not care what happened to the other men on base. And if a man were on second and another on first, you hit the ball so as to get on first, and if the man on second were forced out because only three men were in at bat, it made no difference to you.

Then, one school term, our athletic instructor divided us into teams and for the first time we started playing for score. Joe, the boy before me, had walked to first and it was my turn at bat. The director came up to me and said, "Now you make a sacrifice hit." "What's that?" I asked. "You bunt the ball so that all they can do is put you out at first. Meanwhile, Joe will make second." I couldn't see it. When the pitcher threw the ball, I just hit it with all my might like I always had. The shortstop fielded it, tossed it to second; he tossed it to first and we were both out.

The coach did not say a thing to me. Nobody else did either. A few innings later I was at bat, hit a single and was on first. I saw the coach talking to the next boy at bat. He bunted the ball, I ran to second, he was out at first. Suddenly I understood. I understood team play where you work for the team and not for yourself alone, and I understood something else, why they call it a sacrifice hit. A man goes up to bat and deliberately gives up his own chance to score so that he can advance another member of the team. This is his sacrifice for the benefit of others.

And many a time since then, when I hear the term "sacrifice hit" I think not only of baseball but of all the other areas of life in which people give up their own chances to swing hard at the ball so that others may move ahead.

Think about it. You have seen it yourself, haven't you? A runner who is not quite good enough to win a race is taught to "pace" the champion so as to keep him up to racing speed. The big day comes, the pacer is out in front. He's running his heart out so that, on the last lap the champ can close the gap, sprint in and win the race and break a record.

Sacrifice hits. Life is full of them. I know a man whose father died prematurely. There was barely enough to keep life together for the mother and two sons. If my friend had wished, he might have left home at seventeen and made his way, but no, he stayed home, got a job, sent his younger brother through medical school, and that brother has triumphed over many an illness. Sacrifice hit, wasn't it?

An artillery spotter goes out into an exposed position to guide his buddy's cannon. A covering man will "draw fire" deliberately to help screen the movements of another. A platoon or company may make a feint on a battlefield to confuse the enemy—sacrifice hits that cost life.

Every time a human being puts his team before himself, whether that team be his family, his faith, his city, his country, he is a sacrifice hitter. All the great men of the ages have been. Moses never entered the Promised Land. He got the team around third base headed toward home, and then went out to die alone. Jonathan had a throne to inherit, but stepped aside before one he knew was a great man. Sacrifice hit. And

23

Isaiah said that all the people of Israel must be the suffering servant, that they make the sacrifice hit by standing up against tyranny and oppression, by practicing justice and mercy, by persisting in spite of all odds, that humanity might thereby be blessed. Sacrifice hit.

I like to see young men on the baseball field. I love the sparkle of spring, the sharp crack of the bat, and the fine feeling of a ball slapping into a glove. But most of all, I love the lesson of baseball that I hope all of us will learn, the lesson of the sacrifice hit. Give of yourself, young men, give of yourselves, all people, that mankind may advance another base.

Rabbi Robert I. Kahn

* * *

Whom to Follow?

Young people claim today that they cannot trust any one over the age of thirty. Why is this? There is unquestionably a great deal of unhappiness on the part of teenagers with the kind of world which their adult generation has given them. It is a world of hate, war, and the danger of destruction. Why should they trust their elders who have made such a mess of a world which could be so wonderful and so beautiful? This

24

feeling is well expressed by a young person:

> We have heard words like "God" and "country" used to whitewash some of the vilest deeds in history. We have been exhorted to honesty by rascals to patriotism by near-traitors. We "know the price of everything and the value of nothing" because all values have been carefully and efficiently destroyed before our eyes. We pin our faith on men because we have not been given a faith in anything bigger, and when men fail, as fail they must, we are left bewildered and hopeless.
>
> We rebel because we want a new order in which a man can stand up in the decency and pride that are his birthright.
>
> Enlightened self-interest seems to be the guiding principle in the lives of many of our elders. And you want us to sweat, to fight, to live for this? Thank you, but we are not interested. Give us a cause big enough to challenge and demand all our energy and spirit. Dare us to take on humanity, to change the world, and then come and help us remake it.

But the warning to young people not to trust anyone over thirty is only a half-truth. It makes a good slogan but not much more. Should we distrust the Leo Baecks, the Martin Bubers, the Albert Schweitzers, the Albert Einsteins of our world? Hardly.

At the same time, young people should be warned that they must not necessarily trust everybody under thirty, nor for that matter under twenty. Much of the unhappiness of young people is due to the fact that their own lives are empty and meaningless. They are close to despair and hopelessness because there is nothing within them which challenges and inspires them. It is easier for them to place the blame on others than to look into themselves for the necessary push to make something of their lives. Many people under thirty waste their lives and sometimes destroy them not only by experimenting with drugs, but also by experimenting with bad companions and activities which undermine the body and the spirit. We see such young people on television, writhing away to the tune of drums and trumpets which have the same effect upon the mind and the soul as do drugs. What bothers me most of all about what I see is not the dance but the faces of the dancers, empty, drained of emotion, drained of any kind of animation. Their hips are alive, but their faces are dead.

For those who desire it, this can be an exciting world. We live in an age of revolution, the revolution of oppressed peoples, of downtrodden races, of a world which seeks a better way than of long wars in which the generation of your parents and grandparents has existed. Yours may be the generation which will achieve the breakthrough into a more decent world, and yours is the opportunity to play a part in the creation of that world. We Jews have always believed that the single individual can play a most important part in his environment. We are told, "He who saves a single soul is as though he has saved the entire world." We are also told, "Each one should regard himself as though the world were balanced in the scales between good and evil. His one act can tip the scales one way or the other."

Young people, as always, are on the look-out for kicks. There is nothing wrong in that. The question is, what kind of kicks are you trying to get out of life? For those who are imaginative and creative, the kicks that you can get are to be found in a world to which you can make a great and lasting contribution. You can get your kicks out of working for the cause of peace. You can get your kicks out of making your contribution to the cause of human equality. You can get them from working on behalf of the renewal and the survival of the Jewish people. You can get your kicks by living in accordance with the ethical and prophetic teachings of our religion, by supporting Israel!

When you do this, you will not worry too much about going along with the crowd. You will find your fulfillment and your companions in the ranks of those who are moving on to a better world, instead of those who stand frozen in this world of which they despair. If you must follow, follow those whose eyes are fixed on the future, not those whose backs are turned to it in fear. If you must follow, follow the people of tomorrow. Do not stand on the sidelines. The sidelines can be a very lonely place when the hope of the world is passing by.

Some people say that God is dead. But the truth is that many people are dead, even while they go to work, tee off on the golf course, or attend a cocktail party. They are dead within. Those who live are the ones who have something to live for. May you be among the living.

Rabbi David Polish

27

A Delight

The Sabbath is given us to have a ball. I mean that. We learn that from the prophet Isaiah (58:13): "V'Karata la-shabbat oneg, and call the Sabbath, and make the Sabbath a delight." In our words, have fun on the Sabbath.

What do we mean by having fun on the Sabbath?

Well, let's take a look at New Year's. Every people celebrates the birth of a New Year. Compare New Year beginning at midnight January 1, and our Rosh Hashanah beginning at sundown usually in September. Paper horns and Ram's horns, the Shofar. Loud beat bands and hushed solemn choirs. Drunkenness in the streets and sobriety in the synagogue. Wild reaching for thrills and serious personal reflection of life's meaning and purpose. Screaming "Happy New Year," and greeting people with "L'shana tova, may you be inscribed for a year of life." Racing irresponsibility on the roads to smash-ups and death, and sitting at worship?

Let's make one thing clear: To be Jewish is to be different, stubbornly different in the approach to life. We are part of humanity, yet we have our own identity. We are part of the American family, yet we are a family of our own. You are citizens of a community, good citizens, but you live in your unique home with its own patterns of life. The hope for a harmonious and interesting humanity is not sameness but variety within unity.

28

We proceed to prepare for the Sabbath celebration. We wash up, we freshen up, some even apply makeup. We change from jeans and sweaters, from skirts and blouses to more dressy attire. The commercials tell us that clothes make the man, and bring out the loveliness of the woman. I'm not 100 percent sure of that, but I think that a change of clothes, from the sloppier to the more elegant, does set off a change of mood.

Washed, kempt, and dressed we approach a ball, a dance. Now, it takes more than one person to have a ball. It takes a collectivity of people, a group, a crowd. So we crawl out of ourselves and join the family, not only physically around the table, but with all our hearts and all our souls and all our might. We catch up with our father, our mother, and our sisters and brothers, if we are blessed to have them. We touch home base and it gives us new strength. It dawns on us that we are not alone. We sense that we belong, that we are wanted, needed, and loved. And for a fleeting moment we think of love, we dream of marriage ahead, of ultimately becoming a parent, presiding royally at the head of a Sabbath table. There is a touch of Cinderella in the opening scene of the Sabbath.

A ball usually means a good meal. Hamburgers, hot dogs, and pizza are seldom seen on the Friday evening Sabbath table. Mother takes a little more time. She adds a touch of love to the soup, the meat, and the dessert. We don't make Kiddush over TV dinners.

The Sabbath ball moves from the family's little palace to the community's larger palace, the synagogue. The circle widens. We crawl a little more out of ourselves and join a wonderful historic Jewish people, so old yet so alive, going back four thousand years yet looking ahead to thousands more. We rejoin the family of Jews, not only physically in the pews, but with exalted spirit in the Sh'ma. It dawns on us that our own little Jewish family is not alone; it is one of five million families across the earth. We sense that we belong, but to what? This Shalom Aleichem. This Barchu. This Sh'ma. This Mi Chamocha. This Va'-anachnu. This Ayn Kelohenu. What are these melodies conveying? What do the lyrics of these hit tunes say at this Sabbath ball? Do they sing and speak to me? Do they rouse the toes of my heart to dance, to get with it?

Ah, now that I start asking such questions I begin drifting away from the crowd, from the family, and I'm starting to crawl into myself again. I am looking within, and this, exactly this, is prayer. The Sabbath ball has two aspects: it propels our sense of belonging to the individual, and moves us to try to understand ourselves.

All our lives we shall struggle with the tension of the one and the many, I and they. The Sabbath provides us training, weekly exercises for that rough, tough lifelong battle of me and the crowd.

Maybe, if I get with those lyrics, if I catch the rhythm, the beat of those centuries old hit tunes, I'll come through O.K., like the people who composed and sang them and danced to them Sabbath after Sabbath in good times and bad, in prosperity and persecution. Like them, like my people before me, I'll probably get kicked around, get a bloody nose, a black and blue shin here and there, but come through.

These melodies, these words, these thoughts have something, some enduring quality. They don't die! They live, and the people who hang on to them live, stay afloat.

The theme of the decorations in the great Sabbath ballroom is an anchor, an anchor sunk in the bottom of history's stormy ocean, an anchor made of the stuff of eternity. Rusty, barnacled, some pieces violently broken off, but there it is—and it holds! And I am walking the decks of the safe, unsinkable ship of the wise.

Let's take a look at that anchor. What is this stuff of eternity? The stuff of eternity is tension, the tension between me and the many. Vigorous life is tension— between love and hate, peace and war, freedom and bondage, wealth and poverty, good and evil. Yes, tension between God and man, and this, exactly this, is faith.

All our lives we shall be pulled this way and that, in a tug of war. If the symbol of the anchor etches itself deeply on our minds, we will not be torn apart, we will hold, for the six days after the ball.

I got a little reflective there for a while, but you brought me back, my Rock and my Redeemer. Now I have a faint glimpse of the sense of responsibility and balance, and of the good feeling of just being at home with myself, and doing the best with each cell you have built into me, my Creator.

Let me recall the memories of my people, let me pray the prayers of my fathers, and their fathers, let me sing the songs of this eternal faith. How good and how pleasant it is, to keep this Sabbath which has kept me and my forefathers, to remember it and to keep it, and to build me a wholesome life of its teachings.

The Sabbath is given us to have a ball. I mean that, we learn that from the prophet Isaiah. "V'karata la-Shabbat oneg, and call the Sabbath, and make the Sabbath a delight."

Rabbi Ely E. Pilchik

* * *

Live It Up

I don't know how far or how fast Mother Goose traveled through the air in her day, but if Mother Goose had lived in 1918 she might have taken a ride in an American Spad plane. If Mother Goose lived today, she could travel through the air in a jet at an amazing speed.

No matter what the speed of the plane, the pilots of commercial airlines are particularly concerned when visibility is zero, and ceiling zero.

Captain Frank Barnes, a pilot, once told of the time when he started out on a routine flight. Visibility was unlimited and ceiling was unlimited. Suddenly fierce winds came up. The plane bounced and rocked up and down, from one side to the other. The sky became darker and darker until both pilot and copilot couldn't

32

distinguish a thing. Knowing they were somewhere near their destination, they looked down hoping to see the field lights on the landing field, but the fog was so thick that they couldn't see anything, not even a flicker of light. Now they were flying blind, depending entirely upon instruments. Captain Barnes worked frantically at the radio, hoping to get instructions from the control tower. But all he could get was muffled static. The radio was dead. The pilot looked at his instruments again, and knew that he was flying in a circle. He hoped and prayed that he was circling the field. If only he could hear a voice to guide him and direct him to safe landing. The stewardess came in to say that the passengers were getting nervous and wanted to know how soon they would land. Captain Barnes told the stewardess that everything was all right, but he knew it was not. The gas was low! Fear began to clutch at his heart. He knew that it was impossible to land without the guiding voice from the control tower. Then, just when he was about resigned to despair, he heard a voice. It was weak but he could hear it and understand it. The voice was directing him to safe landing, even though he was flying blind, even though visibility was zero, and ceiling zero.

We are not pilots, and we don't have to worry about landing a jet, but at some time or another, we all fly blind, with visibility zero and ceiling zero. Often we can't see a thing, ahead or above. Everything seems wrong and dark, and we long for a voice telling us what to do, a voice that would guide and direct us to safe landing.

In the Book of II Kings, Chapter 19, verses 11–12,

we learn that the prophet Elijah felt that way. Everyone seemed to be against him. The queen Jezebel had threatned to have him killed, and so he escaped for his life, hiding in the hills, in caves, not knowing where to go or what to do. When he was about ready to give up, feeling that visibility was zero and ceiling zero, he climbed the mountain top, and there he prayed that he might be able to see the presence of God. "And behold, a great and strong wind rent the mountain and broke in pieces the rocks, but the Lord was not in the wind. And after the wind an earthquake, but the Lord was not in the earthquake. And after the earthquake a fire, but the Lord was not in the fire. And after the fire, a still, small voice."

When Elijah heard the voice he knew that he was no longer walking or flying blind. He had someone to help and guide him, at last visibility was unlimited, and ceiling unlimited. He could see his way into the future, the way that would lead him to God.

The same voice that spoke to Elijah can speak to us. When we feel that everything is wrong and dark and we don't know what to do, when we are afraid, and frightened, unhappy, or ashamed, then we have to turn the knobs of our hearts and tune in to God. When we do, we shall hear a still, small voice, the voice of conscience that will tell us how to avoid the wrong way, and how to choose the right, the voice that will steer us throughout our life.

When Judaism summons us "to live it up," it means to elevate our lives, our thoughts, and our deeds to the highest ideals and to the loftiest principles of our religious faith. In that way, we turn ourselves in the direction of the Most High and "live it up"—to God.

Rabbi William B. Silverman

* * *

The Case of the Missing Rabbi

There once was a rabbi whose students loved him so greatly that they came to believe something strange and wonderful about him. What and why they believed as they did needs explanation.

Although the rabbi was with them every day of the week, teaching the wisdom of Judaism, he would quickly leave them each Wednesday at noon. Even if he was in the middle of a lesson, explaining the Torah, translating and clarifying difficult texts of the Talmud, he would depart each Wednesday as the clock struck twelve. His abrupt departure was odd. He uttered no word, no "Pardon me." He simply shut the books and was gone.

The students used to speculate about this disappearance of their rabbi. Where did he go? What did he do? He was in such a hurry that his mind seemed to be shut to any other thought but what he was about to do. From teaching them he left to do something which must have had even greater significance to him.

He was usually such a pleasant, kindly, thoughtful

man. He was gentle and never scolded when they made an error or were not properly prepared. Patiently he would go over their lesson. Calmly he would go over the text, the thought, the teaching, and when he talked his voice was beautiful to hear, and his explanations were vivid and unforgetable.

The students guessed about his departure. One said, "He goes home to rest, for the work is difficult and the teaching exhausting." Another declared, "He probably has to meet with other rabbis to discuss the Jewish life of the community." Still another insisted, "Our rabbi has gone to his study to enrich his own mind in order to teach us." Then somebody said, "I know where he goes. Where else would such a holy, saintly man go but to visit with God in Heaven." "Yes, yes," the others shouted, "You are right. Our Rabbi leaves us each Wednesday for Heaven." And this is what they came to believe. They began to look upon him with special awe and love. Such a holy man! Such a saint! Of course he goes to Heaven!

One day a student from another city was visiting with the class and their rabbi. It wasn't long before the students told him of their amazing idea about their teacher. But this young man laughed at them. He said, "In the first place, a person must die to go to Heaven; and in the second place, you fools, let me tell you that there is no Heaven." They were shocked and turned from him. Such a skeptic, such a disbeliever they could not accept, for they were certain about Heaven and convinced that their rabbi went to Heaven each Wednesday afternoon.

The skeptic then argued, "Listen to me. Tomorrow is Wednesday, I'll hide behind the big tree outside this classroom and when your rabbi leaves, I will follow him. I will see where he goes, and then come back and tell you whether or not your teacher goes to Heaven." Somewhat shaken by his scheme, they were silent until one of them said, "Very well, do as you have planned."

The next day, the skeptic hid behind the big tree and was laughing to himself, "What fools, what idiots these students are! I'll show them. I'll prove to them how mistaken they are." All at once the rabbi appeared and the pursuit began. First the saintly rabbi went to the grocery store and purchased food. Then he went to the woods and picked up small logs. All these he placed in a huge bag which he apparently carried easily, although it was heavy.

The skeptic then watched the rabbi as the holy man went to the homes of the poor and left them food which they needed so much, and wood to keep their fireplaces burning. The skeptic followed the rabbi who went to the town's little hospital to cheer the sick, to the jail to bring a word of faith to the prisoners, and to the homes of mourners to express a word of comfort to the bereaved.

The next morning as the skeptic came to the school the pupils crowded around him beside the big tree, "Tell us," they clamored, "Tell us if it is true. Doesn't our rabbi go to Heaven, doesn't he? Tell us! Tell us!" The skeptic was silent for a long while. The students were frightened. They could not imagine why he did not speak. "What is wrong?" they cried, "Tell us. Tell us!'' And then, very quietly, in a still voice the skeptic replied, ''Heaven? Did you say Heaven? Higher than that, oh, so very much higher!''

Rabbi Hyman Judah Schachtel

* * *

The Two Artists

There was once a king who built a beautiful palace. In the palace were two magnificent halls, one facing the other. The king decided to have the halls decorated and ornamented by the two leading artists in the land. He called them in and explained to them that each was to use his own judgment and skill in the work of ornamentation, and that on the day of dedication he would reward each of them according to his labors. One of the artists was very diligent and faithful to his task and went to work immediately, decorating and beautifying his hall. The other, no less skilled than his colleague, had a tendency to be lazy. He did not begin immediately, but kept on finding excuses to delay his work to another day. Months passed by and he had accomplished nothing. When the day of dedication drew near, the lazy artist realized that he would have to go to work with superhuman energy if he was to complete his task.

He went to the palace and looked into the hall that was decorated by his colleague. As he admired its magnificence, he realized that he could never produce anything comparable to it in the short time that was left. Not knowing what to do, he put a mirror behind the curtain that separated one hall from the other so that the work of his colleague was reflected in the mirror when the curtain was pulled aside. The dedication came. Kings and nobles from many lands were present, and the king proudly took them first into the hall that had been decorated by the hard-working artist. The king then explained that there was a second hall of the same size and shape behind the curtain and that another artist had been commissioned to decorate this hall.

He pulled aside the curtain, and everyone beheld in the second hall an exact replica of the first. The king alone realized that subterfuge and deceit had been used.

The next day he called the two artists before him and said, "I promised that I would reward you in accordance with your labors."

Pointing to a chest of gold and jewels standing near the end of the decorated hall, he said to the hard-working artist, "This is your reward." Then he pulled aside the curtain and, pointing to the reflection of the chest of jewels in the mirror, he said to the other artist, "This is your reward."

Rabbi Joseph Klein

* * *

He Saved His Energy

Manfred Cohen was born in Germany. When the Nazi power was triumphant, his parents and he were compelled to flee. His parents went to South Africa, and he was fortunate enough to land in England. While he was attending school in England, World War II broke out. Manfred recognized that he had a definite obligation—to enlist in the British Army, to defend the country which had given him asylum, and to take up arms against the tyranny which had expelled him and his dear ones from his native land. He enlisted in the Royal Air Force, and was stationed on the east coast of England to guard against attacks by enemy planes and against Nazi attempts to land during the night by submarines. One day while he was on patrol, he observed the conning tower of a submarine. It had already been spotted by British reconaissance planes which were diving over it and dropping their bombs on it. The submarine was hit. It struggled to the surface, and its sailors scrambled out of the hatches. After a few minutes, only one sailor seemed to be strong enough to combat the surf, and was swimming in the waters about a half of a mile off shore. It was apparent that he could not last much longer. He was afraid to try to swim toward England, and it seemed certain that he would drown. Although he wore lifesaving equipment, it was apparent it would not hold him up too long.

Manfred Cohen was a strong swimmer, a lifesaver. What should he do? There in distress in the sea was a

Nazi whose people had inflicted horrible cruelties upon him and had nearly put his parents to death. The man was also an enemy of his adopted country. Should he brave the surf and try to save the rascal, or should he just let him drown? Manfred did not debate. He forgot that the man in the sea was a foe. He forgot what his people had done to him and his family. He saw a human being in distress. He plunged into the waters of the sea, swam out to the Nazi, and brought him safely to the English shore. Thus did this Jewish lad save the life of an enemy of his country and an enemy of Judaism.

When asked subsequently why he did it, Manfred replied, "I remembered reading on Yom Kippur, the most sacred day of our faith, the story of Jonah. Jonah did not want to save Nineveh because its people were enemies of his. But Jonah was forced by God to go and save them. This he did. Saving an enemy is God's will, Jonah learned. This is a Yom Kippur reading, because Judaism regards the obligation to help all human beings, even our foes, as essential. Service to the children of God is the highest Jewish call. So, moved by these teachings of my faith, I plunged into the surf, and I saved the enemy of my people and of my religion. I believe that this is Judaism."

Rabbi Ferdinand M. Isserman

* * *

A Story of Two Little Pine Trees

Two little pine trees grow gracefully and silently, as all little pine trees do, on the lawn in front of my house on Cape Cod. Often I sit in a chair lazily observing these two little trees. They give me much pleasure.

Cape Cod, as you probably know, makes up the eastern part of Massachusetts. It reaches out into the Atlantic Ocean, shaped like an arm from the elbow to the fingers. There are many pine trees on the Cape. They are usually described as "scraggy," that is, tall and lean, with no branches at all on the lower part of the trunk and only some branches on the top. Although these branches hold pine needles and cones, they cast no shade at all, for they are too thin, too lean, and too high up. But they are tough. Powerful winds and frequent storms sweep over the Cape, and the trees sway and bend and sometimes lose some of their top branches. You can always see some of these broken branches hanging way up in the air, as though saying to the storms, "You can't get me down!" One such broken branch has been hanging from the top of a tree in front of my house, facing the little pine trees I want to tell you about, for some three or four years, and won't let go.

There are many small pine trees all over the Cape. They belong to the pine tree family but they are short, have many branches, and are loaded with green needles and cones. There are quite a number of them in the back of my house. They seem to like to grow close to each other. There were no little pine trees in front of my house, and the small lawn was rather bare and, I thought, a bit lonely looking.

One day I dug up two small trees from the back of the house and planted them in front, a little to the side of the house, about four or five feet apart. I was advised to give them plenty of water for some weeks and then let them take care of themselves. Pine trees do take care of themselves and don't require much attention. In fact, if you give them too much attention you only hurt them.

For some weeks I watered these transplanted little trees and they seemed to be adjusting to their new place. One of them especially seemed to grow. It was green, and began growing two cones. The second one too seemed to thrive, but not as well. Its top branches began to droop, looking down instead of up, and the little tree began to lean away from its partner. After a while I noticed that the first tree too began to bend away from its companion tree. It was a foolish picture: two trees, very much alike, only a few feet apart, looking as if they were angry and refuse to have anything to do with each other. I kept watering them, hoping that they would straighten out and create a more friendly picture, but they would not. Instead, they kept leaning further and further away from each other.

The time came for me to close the house for the winter and return to the city. I was unhappy about leaving those little trees in their silly positions, so I took a heavy string, tied it to the two trees and pulled them toward each other, thus making them stand straight. Then I left the Cape for the winter.

We have cold winters. Many times in the course of

43

the winter, as the blizzards raged and heavy snows fell, I wondered how the two little trees were getting along. Were they standing up straight, or did the heavy snow bend them more and more away from each other?

The next summer, when my family and I were driving back to the Cape, we talked about the trees and kept asking ourselves whether they were still there. Were they firmly rooted in the ground and were they producing new branches and new green needles? And, especially, were they still angry at each other?

I think I drove the car a little faster than I ordinarily would as we came closer to our house. The first thing we saw were the two trees. There they were in front of our house, firmly rooted, green and erect as trees can be. The heavy string I had tied was hanging loose from one of them. The trees seemed to say, "We don't need help any more. We leaned on each other; we helped each other stand up straight. We came through the winter in fine shape. See how straight and green we are? And do you notice the new cones we are growing?"

That's why all summer I watched these two little pine trees with much pleasure and felt very peaceful. I know it will be a pleasure to observe them next summer.

Rabbi Beryl D. Cohon

* * *

You Should Take It With You

On an autumn day the great Rabbi Israel Shem Tov once visited a town in his district in Eastern Europe. The people were overjoyed at his coming and asked if he would like to see the local synagogue. Naturally, he said he would be happy to see their prayer- and school-house. When they arrived, the famous teacher was invited to be the first to enter the building. The door was fully open and the doorway very wide. Still the renowned sage stood there, seemingly held back by some invisible barrier against which he appeared to be pushing with all his strength.

Finally he turned to the people and said, "I can't get in. It's too crowded in there."

"Crowded?" the people asked in astonishment, "why that's impossible! No one is in there. There hasn't been anyone inside since the Holy Days."

"That's just what I mean," said the Baal Shem, "Don't you see, from wall to wall and from floor to ceiling your sanctuary is full of all the prayers you have uttered here. I am sure that your classrooms are still full of all the Torah you've learned there. This isn't where they belong. You should have taken them out with you. They weren't meant to crowd the synagogue. They were meant to beautify your community, your homes, your hearts. . ."

The people understood. Our people usually do.

I hope you, too, understand that what you learn in our religious school is not intended to remain here.

Take with you what you learn, cherish it always and use it to light the path of your life.

Rabbi Albert S. Goldstein

* * *

Difficult, But Worth the Effort

"It is hard to be a Jew" is one Yiddish saying. Another is: "It is good to be a Jew." Are both true? Can the difficult still be good? Yes.

First let us understand why it is hard. A Greenland Eskimo once helped a group of Americans to reach the North Pole. He was rewarded with a free trip to New York City. When he returned to his native village, he told of igloos that touched the clouds, of strings of houses with people living in them moving along tracks, of fireless light, and of many other miracles in the white man's land. From that moment people never called him by his right name any more; to the day he died, still in disgrace, he was called Sag-dluk, the Liar.

When Knud Rasmussen traveled from Greenland to Alaska, his Eskimo guide was Mitek. Mitek visited Copenhagen and New York and was dazzled by what he saw. When he returned home, he decided to avoid the fate of Sag-dluk. So he told his fellow villagers how he and Dr. Rasmussen kept a kayak in New York and paddled out each morning on the Hudson to hunt the plentiful seals there. In the eyes of his countrymen Mitek is a very honest man and his neighbors treat him with deep respect.

The road of the teller of new truths has always been rocky. Elijah had to flee for his life. Jeremiah was thrown into a quicksand pit. Akiba was skinned alive. Socrates was forced to drink poison. Bruno was burned at the stake for teaching that God is one. Galileo was forced to deny the truth that the earth moved around the sun. Gandhi was assassinated by one of his own countrymen whom he tried to enlighten and set free. History's pages are crimson with the blood of truth seekers. New ideas are seldom welcome. People who teach such ideas are often made to suffer. It is hard to be bearers of light to people who prefer their more familiar darkness. That is why it is hard to be a Jew.

H. G. Wells tells of an explorer who disappeared in the Brazilian jungle while searching for a lost tribe. This scientist stumbled and fell through an opening in the earth. Deep below he discovered the descendants of the lost tribe. Generations before they too had tumbled down this same long slope. Living so long in utter darkness they had become totally blind.

There is a proverb: "In the country of the blind, the one-eyed man is king." With two good eyes, the scientist naturally expected the blind people to make him their guide. He was in for a shock. Not only did they not invite his help; they thought his eyes were disgusting wounds in his face and regarded his talk about "seeing" as a sign of insanity. Indeed they refused even to let him live among them unless he agreed to undergo an operation to remove his eyes.

Did he permit their blind surgeons to make him blind? No, he risked his life to save what the inhabitants considered a deformity but what he knew was a priceless blessing.

It is not easy to be different. But if the difference lies in having vision, then whatever we pay to keep it is worth the cost.

It was not easy to be an Elijah, a Jeremiah or an Akiba; a Socrates, a Bruno, a Galileo or a Gandhi, but it was good for the world to have them. It was their mission and their glory to light the path of mankind as, step by step, we mount upward from the dark caverns of ignorance and superstition toward the shining stars of truth. Yes, it is hard to be a Jew. But it is also good.

Rabbi Albert S. Goldstein

* * *

The Religious Reason

The Jerusalem Talmud tells us that when Rabbi Joshua went to Rome, on his first day there he found in the street a magnificent piece of jewelry. No sooner did he pick it up than he heard a court herald announcing in the public square: "The princess has lost a most valuable jewel. She offers a portion of gold as a reward for its immediate return. Anyone in whose possession it is found after thirty days will suffer capital punishment.'' The Rabbi listened, and then pocketed the jewelry. He kept it with him for a full month and only thereafter did he go to the palace of the princess to return her treasure.

So delighted was she to have it back that she did everything she could think of to excuse him. ''You have undoubtedly just come to Rome, Sir,'' she said. ''No,'' said Rabbi Joshua. ''Then you have just found my jewel.'' ''No,'' said Rabbi Joshua. ''Then you did not know I offered a reward . . .'' ''My dear Princess,'' said Rabbi Joshua, ''I knew very well I would have received much gold if I returned it earlier and that I risk grave penalties for my delay.'' ''Then why . . .?'' she asked dumbfounded.

''I do this neither in hope of reward nor in fear of punishment, but only because it is the will of my God whose Torah commands: 'Thou shalt surely bring back unto thy neighbor every lost thing which he has lost and thou has found.' (Deut. 22:1–3)''

This should be the only religious motivation for ethical conduct: not fear of being found out, or the penalty in such painful discovery; not hope of reward either here or hereafter; but the high joy of the knowledge that you do what is good and right because this is the will of the God of goodness and righteousness.

Rabbi Albert S. Goldstein

* * *

Little Bears for Little Men

The strongest man in ancient Greece got that way by lifting a newborn calf and walking with it on his shoulders as far as he could. On the first day he carried it several yards. Each day thereafter he carried the growing heifer a few feet farther than he was able to do the day before. Five years later he could tote the full-grown cow several miles.

Some people waste their lives waiting for the big moment, the perfect hour, for exactly the right time to do something spectacular, memorable, earth-shaking. They are going to become world-famous (at least, very important) as author, artist, statesman, philanthropist, or prophet, some day. When? Well, it all depends on when you ask them. If they are now fifteen, why it will be when they are twenty-one, or when they finish college, or when they are, at most (say) thirty. If they are already thirty, then it will be when they make their first million. Some day.

They don't realize that the big opportunities come to those who prepare for them, by seizing all the small opportunities, performing the little tasks that lie before them, whatever their hands find to do, with all their might.

Two Ozark Mountain ''boys'' were sunning themselves in a meadow at the edge of a forest. One of them was a hulking giant. The other was a runt, fascinated by the huge size and apparent strength of his companion.

''Ah declare,'' said the fellow, ''you sure are some

hunk o' man! Do you know what Ah'd do if Ah wuz big and strong as you?"

A faint smile and nod showed that the other was awake and listening.

"Why," the little one continued, "Ah'd go to into them thar woods and cotch me the biggest b'ar in it. Ah'd grab 'im lim' from lim'—just to show what a man Ah am!"

Slowly the big fellow turned. "Little man," he said, "there are plenty of little bears in that forest."

Rabbi Albert S. Goldstein

* * *

The Important "Finals"

Zusia was the saintly and adored spiritual leader of a devout congregation of East European hasidim. Like all the pious hasidim, Zusia's mood was usually one of joy. But once he appeared depressed, almost melancholy. To his worried disciples he explained:

"I am concerned about the verdict when I leave this world and you, my beloved students, and stand before the Great Judge. He will not ask me: 'Why were you not like Moses, or Isaiah, or Hillel, or Maimonides?' He knows that He did not bless me with their prodigious gifts. What disturbs me is that I am certain He will ask

51

me: 'Why were you not Zusia? Why were you not your own full self, all you could have been, using the wealth of gifts and capacities which you did have? With all your earthy limitations, but still made in My image, you had an immense divine potential.' "

Anyone who can answer for himself Zusia's question need have no anxiety for the fate of his own external soul; he will pass with flying colors the really important "Finals."

Rabbi Albert S. Goldstein

* * *

You're the Witness

"You are My witnesses," saith the Lord, "and I am God." Rabbi Isaac explained: If you are My witnesses, then I am God. But if your conduct and character give no evidence that I am present and functioning in your life, then for all practical human purposes, I am not God; I might just as well not exist.

God needs your testimony; the evidence your life can bring to bear in proof of the truth of your religion.

Willy-nilly, you are God's witness. To your neighbor, Jew or Gentile, to all the members of your family and everyone who knows you, you are proof of the influence that religion can have on human behavior.

When our people were commanded to build the Tabernacle in the wilderness, God said its purpose was to enable Him to dwell among them. He did not say: "Build me a sanctuary so that I may dwell therein," but "so that I may dwell among them," in the midst of this people.

The Jewish sanctuary was never meant to contain God, but to radiate Him. The true sanctuary is the individual, the person who becomes a dwelling place of the Divine, who witnesses by his conduct and character that he is fashioned in the image of the living God. May each of you become such a sanctuary.

Rabbi Albert S. Goldstein

* * *

How People Change

Did you ever look at a friend whom you hadn't seen for some time and say, "My, how he's changed!" You are impressed with the changes in his appearance, mannerisms, attitudes, and conduct. The changes seem strange.

People do change as they go through life, don't they? Sometimes they change for the worse, and that makes us sad. And sometimes they change for the better, which makes us glad.

53

In the story of Jacob and his "wrestling match" with an angel, or a mysterious figure, or a messenger of God, whichever it was, we read of a man who became so different that his old name was replaced with a new one. It was a sudden shift, literally overnight.

Of course, you know what I am referring to. It is in the Book of Genesis. Jacob did not get along with his twin brother, Esau. First, Jacob bought his brother's birthright so cheaply it was ridiculous, for a bowl of soup. Esau was the first-born and that counted for much long ago. Then, one day, he came home very hungry and found Jacob cooking soup. So he sold all the privileges that went with having been born first for a mess of pottage, as we say. In a way, that wasn't very nice of Jacob, was it?

After that, to make things worse, Jacob (with the help of his mother Rebecca) fooled his old, blind father, Isaac, by dressing up like Esau and getting the best blessing which Isaac had really been saving for Esau.

Now Essau was really angry, so much so that he wanted to kill Jacob, or at least Jacob thought so, and he ran away. He stayed away for fourteen years or more. He married, became wealthy, and wanted to return home.

That was when the great alteration came over Jacob so that his very name had to be changed. In the night he met the mysterious stranger who would not let him go; but Jacob was strong and it came his turn not to let the stranger go. At this point the visitor said, "Your name will no longer be Jacob but Israel, because you wrestled with God and won."

54

That was a sudden switch, or so it seemed. But really not so. Jacob had been getting ready for a new life and destiny for a long time. He had worked hard and learned much since his youth when he had fooled his brother. Now he wanted to make it up to his brother somehow, to be a better person than he had been, more considerate, kinder.

You see, change may seem to come suddenly to people. They get rich quickly, or poor. They lose their good health through accident or disease. They win "fame and fortune" overnight, we think. Outwardly that is true.

But inwardly, inside themselves, in their hearts and thoughts, in their attitudes and manners, in their ideals and ideas, the changes which we think have happened suddenly had really been developing over a long period.

It takes effort, and study, and work, and determination to grow in character. It takes achievements that make us happy, but it also takes trials and failures and disappointments to become "bigger" people. Judaism asks us to work, to study, to face life and wrestle with all the known and unknown forces so that eventually our names will be changed for the better, our reputation for good, and our lives for greater blessing.

Rabbi Joseph R. Narot

* * *

In Three Cities

Modern studies of the human mind tell us that the mind itself is an isle of consciousness about which and below which surges the "Red Sea" of the unconscious. Here broken wishes, unfulfilled desires, and dynamic drives, pound or lilt against the isle of consciousness. In this Red Sea all too often we "seek to drown sorrows which unfortunately have learned how to swim."

Answers to our problems may come from the past.

Take for example three statements emerging from the distant hills of three ancient cities of the Mediterranean world.

The first of these came from the setting of Athens, the capital of culture in the world of Greece. In Athens was a sculptor, a poor one financially, perhaps artistically. It is said that he brought more notoriety than bread to his wife and children. He was a man of ungainly figure, baldness of head, deep-set eyes, thickened lips and snubbish nose. He believed himself guided by an inner voice, and turned his attention exclusively to the study of man.

In his day, Athens was filled with many gods and about this character, Voltaire puts into one of his plays, "There goes an Atheist, he believes in only one God!" This Greek may have given us his last words through his disciples, but his most living words are still quoted daily, if not hourly, for he was a philosopher in the maturity of centuries and contributed a mint of thought with a mite of words. The man was Socrates and his simple words were, "Know Thyself."

In the mid-Mediterranean world was another city with its hill-tops rung with pageantry and beauty. This was not merely the capital of a culture, but the very hearbeat of the ancient world. In Rome lived a man who was a philospher primarily, even though he was an Emperor. He was a strong warrior who repelled invasions, extended imperial frontiers and crushed rebellions. He was also a great builder, but his love of learning was never satisfied. His studies were vast and included metaphysics, jurisprudence, music, poetry and painting. He is best known neither for his imperial armies, his colossal structures, his vast victories or extensive domains, as he is for his simple *Meditations*. He is none other than Marcus Aurelius, Emperor of Rome, who from all his dominions of peoples and domains of thought contributed to his world and ours a simple, yet summary statement, "Control Thyself."

In the area of the crescent of fertile land that is touched by the rim of the desert on the one side, the shores of the Mediterranean on the other, and that is crowned by a capital of the spiritual world, lived another sage. He is as much a guidepost for the twentieth century, as he was for early days. For, in ancient Judea, crowned by the quest of the spirit and gowned by the starlit horizon, lived a shepherd who was later a king. He was greater as a writer, and he drew more nourishment for his people from his shepherd musings than his kingly decrees and his princely wars. He is said to have been a generous spirit; he is known to have become a great warrior and a national hero. He founded a dynasty, established a crown-city, and left his imprint on anything he touched, not only for his life, but for the life of Israel.

His name was David and his occupations were soldiery, poetry, and kingship. It is not David, but the Psalms that speak to us. It is not Israel's king, but Israel's sweet singer to whom we hearken when he pleads, "Judge the poor and the fatherless; do justice to the afflicted, rescue the poor and the needy." In a word he pleads, "Give Thyself."

Thus, when we learn, "Know Thyself," we may practice "Control Thyself," and then be prepared for "Give Thyself." Thus it is that a philosopher's last words, and probably his last moments are "Know Thyself;" that an Emperor's finest words in his fullest luxuries are "Control Thyself;" and the poet's best notes in his greatest songs are "Give Thyself." These indeed are simple statements: "Know Thyself," "Control Thyself," "Give Thyself," but they were gathered from three of the "four corners of the earth." They came from Athens, Rome, and Jerusalem, and speak to us of the twentieth century, even as do the fragments of immortality we find in these ancient communities, when we blow the dust off and polish the pieces anew, so that they may serve our day, as their day, not as stumbling blocks, but as stepping stones from our own confusion to a new era of our fondest hopes in abiding peace within us and about us.

Rabbi Martin M. Weitz

* * *

God Is Good

What is the threefold role of the modern synagogue? It is, to be sure, a house of prayer, or as we say in Hebrew, a beth tefillah. It is also a house of instruction, a beth midrash, where the rabbi is a teacher. And it is a house of assembly, or beth kneseth, the gathering place for family and friends.

What is prayer? Is it not conversation with God? We talk and God listens. Then God speaks to us in a still, small voice, and we listen. The Bible tells us, "Be still and know that I am God."

What is learning? Is it not knowledge leading to wisdom? A new word, a new idea, a new point of view. Who is a wise man? The rabbis say he who learns from everybody.

A little lad, too young for school, was playing with his blocks on the floor of his home. The blocks contained some pictures, and the letters of the alphabet. Somehow the boy spelled out the word G-O-D. His mother told him that this word was God. But when she was asked, "What is God?" she was in trouble. Thereafter the blocks were mixed up and spelled out the word G-O-O-D. The mother saw a light, and told her son, "Why, God is Good, and Good is God." She was right. When we leave each other and say "good-bye," that is another way of saying, "God be with you." At last the mother said, "One more word. Try it again." This time the boy spelled out the words GO-DO. This is what we mean by religious or social action. Not only to recite the Ten Commandments and the Golden Rule, but to Go and Do something about it.

So a religious person should do something about poverty, disease, crime, prejudice and war. He will work through the synagogue to improve society. He will advise the United States Government of his views.

The Hebrew prophets believed in action. In addition to speaking about good and evil, they did something about it. They influenced the people, and dared to speak out against rulers who were unjust and cruel. The spirit of the prophets remains with us to this very day.

What the Jew believes is important. How the Jew behaves is far more important. Who shall ascend the mountain of the Lord? Who shall stand in God's holy place? Only he who has clean hands and a pure heart.

Let this be the generation of those who would seek God's presence. And may God shower His blessings upon you.

Rabbi Charles Mantinband

* * *

The Real Thing

One morning when I went to my door to get the newspaper I saw a headline screaming the news of a tragic fire which had raged in a downtown apartment house, causing the death of eighteen people, including three little children. When I read further into the article for the details, I learned that when the fuse box was examined a copper penny was found in one of the fuse plugs instead of the proper fuse. The newspaper ran a special editorial pleading with the public to take the safety measure of using the proper fuse and not to substitute a coin.

Of course the news shocked me and the editorial impressed me, but I could not help taking this story as a perfect illustration for what we have been saying from the pulpit these many years. When we understand the principle behind the use of the proper fuse it all becomes very clear to us. It is true that the fuse, like the penny, establishes the contact of metal with metal to complete an electrical circuit. The difference is, however, that when the load of the circuit becomes too great and wires would begin to burn, the fuse is so arranged that it "blows" and all electrical current is stopped from passing through. When the wires become overheated and begin to burn, the metal of the penny is a good conductor of the current and thus increases the danger.

We, as a people, very often not so pious or conscious of our religion and cultural inheritance, find what we think are substitutes for religion and culture in our lives. We try to insert the copper penny of philanthropy or charity as token membership to organizations. We try to soothe our conscience by buying our way out. This practice if used consistently can cause the destruction of our people.

61

We must have the safety measure of using the proper fuse of continued study and observance of our heritage to insure that Judaism will go on from one generation to another without interruption.

Rabbi Richard C. Hertz

* * *

Are Jews Different?

Back in the days of the Purim story, we read how the wicked Haman whispered into the ears of King Ahasuerus that "there is a certain people who are different and have separate laws, neither do they keep the king's laws; therefore let them be killed. . . ." Ever since that time, people have wondered about the Jews.

Are we Jews different? Why do some people think so?

We worship one God instead of two or three. Does that make us different? We do not accept Jesus as the Messiah or "the Christ." We do not worship in a church but in a temple. We have separate days for our holidays, like Rosh Hashanah and Yom Kippur, Pesach, Sukkot and Shauvot. We keep the Sabbath day on Saturday instead of Sunday.

Does all this make us different? Not really!

Judaism teaches that underneath, all human beings, regardless of race or color or creed, are children of the One God. And if all have the same Father, we must all be brothers.

Judaism teaches us to love our neighbor as ourselves.

Judaism teaches us to practice honesty, justice, mercy, lovingkindness, and charitableness.

Judaism teaches us that we are good citizens if we cherish liberty, defend freedom, preserve democracy, and pursue paths of peace.

Yet some stupid, prejudiced people who don't like Jews and prevent them from getting certain jobs or living in certain neighborhoods think Jews are "different." They dislike those who are unlike themselves.

Purim has a serious message for our times, beside the fun and merriment and masquerading. Purim comes to remind Jews and all other peoples that Hamans never disappear. They keep bobbing up time and again to persecute our people and pervert freedom. From Purim we Jews learn a great lesson of pride in our people. Though we have to live with the Hamans who come to trouble us now and again, we know we have to live proudly, with self-respect, with dignity. We know we must stand up for the right. We bow down to no one! We know in our own hearts that we are not different from other people except that we worship God in the Jewish way and our Christian neighbors worship Him in the Christian way. But there is only one God! We know that we go to temple, they go to church. But all are houses of God, sacred and holy when people practice outside what they hear preached inside. We know that we say some prayers in Hebrew, like the Sh'ma; they say some prayers in Latin. But prayer in any language is holy if it is sincere and from the heart.

We Jews know we are not "different" unless we become indifferent to God, Torah, or the Jewish people. We believe God created all human beings equal. We remember the story the ancient Rabbis used to tell. Why, asked the old Rabbis, did God take Adam, the first man, from the dust of the north, south, east, and west? So that all four quarters of the earth would be represented, so that no descendants might ever boast, "My ancestors are better than your ancestors and I am better than you." All are equal in the sight of God.

This is the great lesson that the Purim story teaches us at this season. God protects us not because we are Jews or because some person calls us "different", but because we are God's children and He is the Father of all people everywhere.

Rabbi Richard C. Hertz

* * *

Success—Sweet or Sour

Success is wonderful, its taste is sweet to our palates and we hope to enjoy it often. We know that success in school means praise and perhaps special privileges at

64

home. Later in life it will most certainly bring public recognition, a better position, and a higher salary. We are aware of these fruits of success as we understand the consequences of failure. A poor report card from school leads to a cut in our allowance, our telephone privileges may be curtailed, and time that was formerly free will now be scheduled for supervised study. In terms of their effect on our lives, these are minor matters compared to the disasters of adult failure which may result in a loss of position or standing in the community. We imagine that success is always sweet while failure brings only despair and disaster. Unfortunately it is not quite so simple. Success can also be destructive.

Every nation has a small elite upon which it believes the future will depend. On some lonely South Sea Island the elite might be the ritual dancers who perform before the deities; from earliest childhood on they will be treated in a special way as they are guided toward this goal. In some lands the elite are the heroes of the world of sports. The population there will riot over the loss of a soccer game, but not over a change of government. In other lands the elite is composed of those trained to think right, not of those who think well, but those whose thoughts are orthodox. So it is in Communist lands where correct and properly timed quotations from Lenin or Marx may be the key to success. This is their elite.

In our land we are slowly forming an elite based upon intellect, on those who think well. At an early stage in life we separate these boys and girls from the rest and set them on a special road mainly dedicated to the sciences;

later in life we will also honor them more than anyone else. These youths will achieve much and will move upward in their chosen fields. This represents a fine change for there was a time when the only person really honored on a college campus was the football star. Now it is possible for a nuclear physicist to achieve the same status. This new attitude is wonderful and seems to be close to Judaism's stress on the intellect. Yet, we cannot overlook the shortcomings of this new pattern of life. The danger is that those picked may become snobs. It is almost natural for a youngster placed in a special class to feel superior to others. Such temptation is difficult to restrain. Judaism has always tried to subdue such feelings of arrogance for it is the task of religion to overcome our natural inclinations. Alongside admonitions to study, it demands: "Do not make learning a crown with which to exalt yourself or a spade with which to dig." None of the heroes of Scripture depend on learning for their stature. We know nothing about the intelligence of Abraham. No one has ever stressed the scholarship of Isaiah, Jeremiah, or Ezekiel, or the lack of it. Biblical students seem to feel that the great prophet, Amos, was illiterate, but he remains a great man who may inspire us and who we can still read with profit.

This is illustrated by a story which circulated in Europe two centuries ago. There was a town in which most of the men were clever and well educated; however, there was also one illiterate. He was a good and kindly man, but he was never able to learn how to pray. Embarrassed, he just stood in the synagogue and did nothing. Finally, someone taught him the alphabet by rote, but as he could not put the letters together into words, he was almost as helpless as before. During the next holiday he again felt lost, but decided to use the little he had learned by reciting the alphabet as he remembered it. Then he asked God to put the letters into the proper sequence to form the prayers he felt in his heart. The prayer was acceptable before God.

The ancient Greek thinker, Plato, believed that the world would be governed best by a philosopher king, by the most gifted intellectual. Late in life the king of Sicily offered him the opportunity to test his idea, so the old man undertook the long ocean voyage to make the grand experiment, but it failed. Total dependence on intellect will fail. Gifts of mind are wonderful but they must be combined with a good heart, ethical feelings, and much more. For these reasons we attend services and spend many years in religious school. Achievements of the mind can only lead to partial success. But combine them with ethical and moral elements, and real success may be attained. It will not only glow to the outer world, but also within ourselves.

A good friend who enjoys mountain climbing told me about an adventure in a western range a few years ago. There were many fine peaks and he was determined to climb some of them. Soon he realized that it might take him a week to reach the top of any single peak, so he decided to concentrate on one peak only. Yet he imagined that he would be able to enjoy marvelous views each step of the way. Reality differed from his notions, for the moment he began to climb, clouds surrounded him and he saw nothing until he reached the top. Only steep rocks were visible on the way, but from the peak he had a marvelous view of dozens of other mountains. Then he wondered if, rather than just reaching one pinnacle, it would not have been better to have climbed half-way up several peaks for he would have seen much more of the range. Yet he realized that there wasn't time to climb any others now and he doubted whether he would ever return to the same place in those mountains.

Many of us who are older have followed exactly the same pattern in our lives; early in youth we decided on one goal, a single peak, and bent our entire efforts to reach the top. While we climbed to the heights of our career, we saw nothing else, just as if we had been surrounded by clouds. If we chose science, law, or medicine, we isolated ourselves from the rest of the world, sometimes even from our family, often neglecting the worlds of beauty, art, and religion. Eventually we reached the top, but once there, felt keenly disappointed, for, like the young mountain climber, we knew nothing of the rest of the world. Our achievement had brought us recognition; perhaps we had made new discoveries in physics, chemistry, or medicine, but even the adulation of others left us dissatisfied for we had missed so much of life. Many men on those envied heights have wished to climb some other peaks and see another area of life, but this remained a wish. One cannot jump from one mountain top to another. They felt too old, and did not have the energy to descend and begin to climb again. But the young should not make the same mistake. We can train ourselves in many areas of life so that we will be at home in the worlds of religion, ethics, theater, literature, music and all the other arts. As our society, and especially our school pushes us in the opposite direction, this choice is hard to make, but it must be made if we seek real success. Progress and achievement will then come in many areas and we will attain outer and inner success.

Scripture in Exodus presents a detailed description of the Sanctuary in the desert. Endless items for this holy place had to be made and every skill and quality of an entire people were used to build it. As brass, gold, silver, wood, linen, wool, and other materials were needed, so were silversmiths, goldsmiths, carpenters, weavers, and hundreds of other skilled people. The Sanctuary could have been simpler and one man could have built it, but the Bible wanted as many qualities and skills as possible to be represented. All of us wish to make small santuaries of our lives. If we follow a single path we shall fail even if it is the road of the intellect, but if we develop all the qualities with which we are blessed then we will build a magnificent Sanctuary of our lives. It can be so. Let it be so.

Rabbi Walter Jacob

* * *

Bored? Lonely?

During the teenage years many walk through life with a pocket full of pictures, photographs of smiling friends in school or camp. If we compare these pictures with our friends as we actually see them, we realize that there is a great difference. The pictures are full of smiles displaying contentment and satisfaction, but the real persons are often frowning and grumpy. Contentment is our ideal and the photographer, through a trick, has managed to capture it for a moment. That is sufficient for him, but not for us. We would like to possess happiness all the time. It is our goal, and it was equally the aim of the Patriarchs whom we know from Scripture. We strive for it but we rarely attain it. What keeps us from contentment? What stands in our way and whose fault is it?

When we were very young we were often excited and the world seemed most interesting to us. Little children arise early in the morning and declare to the world, ''I'm up, isn't it wonderful'' and they always find it so. If a birthday is a few days off, the youngsters are happily nervous until that day has come. A bit of that feeling will stay with us throughout our life as we long for birthdays, parties, or dances.

At the other end of life people often don't care whether the next day comes or not for they feel that it will be just like the one before. Should it bring surprises, they are sure they will be unpleasant. Some are bored with life and have seen enough, so they just drift from one day to the next.

Strange as it may seem some of us become old very soon in this respect. At fourteen or fifteen some of us get bored and acquire the feeling that "all is vanity." Dullness destroys our contentment. Yet, what do we do about it? When we are bored, we complain and discuss it. Complaint is fashionable and we thrive upon such conversation. We sit in our classrooms or later in life in our meeting rooms or offices and demand that the world excite us. We want someone to stimulate us, to prod us, and to make our life interesting again. We yawn at the world around us. When we face boredom in this way, it is really a commentary upon us, not on the world, for we have displayed a lack of imagination. Boredom is not a condition but a reaction to our own lack of imagination. When hungry, we do not wait for someone to offer us food; we help ourselves. When in pain, we do not wait for a doctor to inquire about our health, but we call him and try to obtain a cure. If we feel that our pay at work is insufficient, we do not await a word from a kindly boss—we ask for a raise or change jobs. We should act upon our boredom too. The dullest meeting or class can allow us time to reflect upon the subject discussed and view it from a new perspective. Then, we may present our thoughts and enliven the session. Boredom can be relieved if we wish it so. When we are bored it is declaration that we have given up and no longer possess the energy to face the world.

Reflect upon Scripture. With the single exception of

Koheleth none of its figures were bored. The word does not exist in the Bible because all its personalities were involved in important endeavors.

In our teen years we not only sometimes taste boredom but also loneliness. Our world is filled with friends with whom we sit in class, walk home, spend weekends and talk for endless hours on the telephone. Yet we often feel lonely. Older people are often troubled by the same feeling, especially after losing someone through death.

Loneliness is a part of all people's lives, as novelists and poets have taught us. We must face it as part of our existence. Even in the midst of a large company it is possible to be lonely. Others may be cheerful, but we are sad. Yet this condition may prove to be a blessing. Solitude is a wonderful gift. Only while alone can we truly be ourselves; only then can we prepare ourselves for more meaningful behavior. Solitude can lead to creativity. It can bring us nearer to God and to our ideals. Naturally, we may wish to share these thoughts with others, but the moment of inception often comes when we are alone.

If we never taste solitude we avoid one of the grandest aspects of life. It is then that we can best study and ponder the challenges which confront us. The heroes of Scripture understood this blessing and valued it. Abraham, Moses, Elijah and Amos were blessedly lonely men who would have agreed with a later poet that "solitude is the audience chamber of God."

In our youth we walk through life with a pocket full of pictures; when we are older we put them on our mantelpiece. We must slowly learn to make use of solitude and overcome boredom. Then we shall see that "solitude is the best nurse of wisdom" and wisdom may be achieved by all those who do not permit themselves to be bored.

Rabbi Walter Jacob

* * *

The Fifth Commandment

"Honor thy father and thy mother that thy days may be long upon the land. . . ."

There was a two-year-old boy who had been taught to obey his parents, to do without question what they demanded of him. Once I visited the home of this boy. I found the father cleaning up pieces of glass that he had accidentally kicked out of a door panel. Suddenly the child appeared, and started for the broken pane with its sharp, jagged edges.

The father ordered, "Stop where you are!"

The boy did stop short, ready to break into tears because of the sudden sharpness of the ordinarily mild voice. Then the father pointed out the glass, and explained that he might have injured himself had he gone on to the door.

The lesson the youngster learned may have saved his life. It certainly kept him from severe injury and

73

bleeding. Honoring his father had assured him long days upon the land.

This incident is reminiscent of a similar story related in an old American reader. In this case the father saw his tiny tot wandering along the railroad tracks. A train was approaching, but the little one seemed not to hear it.

The father shouted, "Lie down flat, son!"

Without further thought the son fell prone. He did not move as the train rolled over him without touching him.

The word of a parent had saved a life.

When children grow unmanageable and refuse to listen to the counsel and warnings of their elders, they are in peril of doing themselves great injury. Often they do not appreciate this truth until they have had children of their own.

Listening to parents is the most important duty of any child. The father and mother seek to protect and improve the child. They tell him to beware of physical and other perils. They object to wrong and hurtful friendships, to neglect of study and other responsibilities, up to the time when they may object to a marriage which they feel will bring misery to their child.

Allowing for all the errors human beings can make, the mistakes of a parent are the rarest of all. Each selflessly seeks the full happiness and success of the young generation.

And that is why the Bible commands the honoring of father and mother. It assures a long and happy life. The religion of Israel, too, is best served by those who follow in the footsteps of those who gave them life.

Judaism's days will be long upon the land only to the extent that children honor the will of God as expressed through the wishes of parents.

Rabbi Abraham Burstein

* * *

A Reward for the Dove

Everyone knows and loves the story of Noah's Ark. But did you ever wonder how even the Ark was big enough to hold two of every kind of animal? Let me tell you the answer: In those days, all the animals were small, no bigger than a cat or a cocker spaniel.

You remember the story, how it rained for forty days and forty nights. At the end of that time, Noah asked for a volunteer from among the fishes to go seek for some dry land.

The salmon spoke up: "Let me go, sir. I am a strong swimmer."

"All right," said Noah. So off went the salmon, heading straight north. After a while he found himself in the bed of what must have been a river. He saw something shiny, a mass of fish-eggs! Puffing himself up to his full width, the salmon hovered over the eggs for days, waiting for them to hatch. And soon they did.

On, on went the salmon, finding more eggs and hatching them, growing wider and fatter at every stop. Soon, he forgot all about Noah and the Ark. Like some people I know, he was so busy minding everybody else's business, he forgot all about his own errand.

When a week passed, and the salmon didn't return, Noah turned to the whale, which was about the size of a big goldfish.

"You look like a sturdy character," said Noah to the whale. "Go, see if you can find some dry land." And with that, Noah dropped him overboard. The whale headed south, and delighted with his new freedom, after the cramped quarters on the Ark, he began spouting water through the hole in his head. After a few hours of playing about, he got a bit hungry. The sea was full of all the fish that the salmon had been so busy hatching. It was fun to chase the little fish and try to catch them.

"I think I'll just have a snack," said the whale, and he gobbled up the fish as fast as he could catch them. Now a whale has a whale of an appetite, so that "snack" went on for hours and days and weeks, until the whale got so enormous that he couldn't swim another stroke, so he just lay on top of the water, fat and lazy, enjoying the sun. He never gave Noah and the Ark another thought. Perhaps you know somebody who is like him, so busy playing and eating that he never gets to his job.

When another week passed and the whale didn't come back, Noah decided to try one of the animals. He reached into the animal pen, and the first animal that he touched was the giraffe, no bigger than a toy. Noah lifted up the giraffe.

"You'll do fine," said Noah. "Go find us some dry land!" With that, he put the giraffe over the side and the little animal began swimming away to the east. On and on he swam, stretching his legs in ever longer strokes, until his legs kept getting longer and longer. After several days, the giraffe lifted his head out of the water and spied a luscious date palm, sticking its head just above the water. The giraffe swam over to the tree, but as he came near, he saw a bigger-looking palm with an even larger cluster of dates, a little farther away. On he went, and as he drew near the second tree, he saw a whole grove of trees ahead of him. Each time he stretched farther out of the water looking for more, his neck got longer. Each time he reached a tree, the next trees looked better. Noah and the Ark were completely forgotten. Some people are just never satisfied with what they have, are they? They always think something else will be better.

Another week had gone by on the Ark. By now, the rainbow was in full glory in the sky. Noah knew that the rain was definitely over, but which way led to dry land? He turned to the big cage filled with birds of every color.

"Which one of you birds will find the dry land for us?" asked Noah.

"Me!" cooed the dove.

Noah opened the cage and the lovely white dove flew onto his finger. Noah carried her up on deck, and off she flew, straight west. Straight on she flew. The sun, which had started out behind her, rose overhead, and finally caught up with her. Just as the sun disappeared into the sea, the little dove spied a bit of land sticking out of the water, and on it was a single olive tree. The dove paused for a few minutes on a branch, broke off a twig in her beak, and headed back toward the Ark.

Just as the morning sun peeped over the eastern horizon, the little bird landed on the deck-rail of the Ark. There was Noah, sound asleep in a chair. The dove dropped the olive-twig in Noah's lap with a happy chirp. Noah awoke with a start.

Stroking the tired bird, Noah said: "Well done, little dove! You have done your task quickly and done it well!" And thinking of the salmon, the whale, and the giraffe, Noah said: "If there were only more people who did their assigned jobs quickly and well, this would be a peaceful world. Little dove, the whole world will know what you have done. Whenever people think of peace, they'll remember you. And whenever they want a picture to represent peace, they will use your picture with that olive branch in your mouth."

And, boys and girls, if you go to the United Nations and see the emblem of peace all over that beautiful building, you'll see Noah's dove with the olive branch in her mouth. And let me ask you one final question: Which do you want to be like: the busybody salmon; the fat, lazy whale; the greedy, dissatisfied giraffe; or the prompt and helpful dove?

Rabbi Malcolm H. Stern

* * *

Don't Cry Over Spilt Milk

In the forests of Eastern Europe there lived a poor man who earned his living by catching wild birds. He sold unusual birds to aviaries or zoos. He plucked the feathers of other birds and sold those bright adornments for women's hats. Catching birds is an uncertain business, so he often was so hungry he had to eat the birds he caught.

Once he had tramped through field and forest a whole day without snaring a single bird. On his way home, tired and discouraged, he visited his last trap. There he found a tiny bird. It was so ordinary he could not sell it to a zoo, its plumage so plain that not a single feather was worth taking, and its body so small that it hadn't a morsel of meat on its bones. He was about to thrust it to the ground, when his startled ears heard these words:

"Don't hurt me. Don't." Yes, it was the bird talking. Well, thought the man, this is a more valuable bird than I realized!

"I won't hurt you," the man said, "I can get a fine price for a bird that talks."

"Please set me free," the bird pleaded, "let me go!"

"You're the only bird I've caught all day. I can't let you go." said the man.

"I know a few secrets that can make you rich and successful." The bird spoke with such ease and assurance that the hunter found himself listening as if it were a human being talking.

"Well, how can I possibly ever be rich and successful

in this miserable bird-hunting business?"

"If you promise to let me go, I'll tell you the secret."

"I promise!" the man said almost before he knew that the words were out.

"Just remember three things: Don't believe everything you hear! Don't attempt the impossible! Don't cry over spilt milk! Now let me go."

The hunter didn't think he had made such a good bargain, but being an honest man, if nothing else, he kept his word and let the bird go.

With that the bird flew to a branch just beyond the reach of the man.

"Ho-ho-ho, what a mistake you made letting me go. You fool! Within my body I carry the world's largest diamond, large as an ostrich egg. If you had kept me you would now be rich. Ho-ho-ho!"

Wild with anger at the taunting bird, the hunter jumped high as he could; but the bird sat cozily, an inch above his outstretched fingers. Filled with an overpowering greed for the lost treasure, the man began climbing the tree, but the bird kept hopping from branch to higher branch, always out of reach. When the bird got to the top of the tree where the branches are thin and unsteady, the hunter lost his balance and tumbled to the ground, bumping all the way down and landing at the foot of the tree with the breath knocked out of him.

The little bird perched herself on the lowest branch and regarded the dazed hunter with a sorrowful eye.

"I'm so sorry I had to do this to you," she sighed, "but it's the only way I could be sure you would remember and follow my lesson.

"I told you that the first secret was: Don't believe everything you hear. Yet the minute I told you something you wanted to believe, even though it was impossible, you believed me. How could I have within me a diamond as large as an ostrich egg, or even the size of a walnut, when I am so very tiny myself? But you were so greedy you believed it.

"The second secret was: Don't do what you know is impossible for you. Even a silly man like you should know you can't catch a bird by climbing a tree after it. Still you placed you life in danger by trying to do what a bird can, but a man can't.

"And last of all, I told you: Don't cry over spilt milk.

"When you've done something that can't be undone, don't waste your time fretting about it. Just resolve to learn from your experience and do better next time.

"You had agreed to let me go. You kept your promise, and that was good. But then, when you thought it was a mistake, you almost killed yourself trying to change what you had properly done.

"So, don't lie there feeling sorry for yourself. Get up and go about your business, and remember my three rules. You will see that this nasty experience will be a great help to you."

With a flit of her tail and a cheerful chirp, the little bird flew off into the forest.

Rabbi Eugene J. Sack

* * *

The Sukkah Speaks to Me

One day little Jimmy fell asleep in the Sukkah. It was not an elaborate Sukkah, but a simple one built right beside his grandfather's house. Jimmy was waiting for his grandfather and he sat in a large chair, listening to the wind blowing through the frail boards out of which the Sukkah had been made. The sounds were like music and Jimmy was very comfortable as he waited to hear the footsteps of his grandfather. Suddenly he was asleep. His chin rested on his chest and he breathed ever so lightly. He began to dream and his dream was about the Sukkah, the wind, the music, the lovely sounds that he heard while he was still awake.

More and more the wind sounded like angels' voices. In fact, Jimmy began to talk with the mysterious singers who answered him sweetly and in a most friendly way. First he heard them sing, "Every hour, every day, 'Thank you' is good to say.'' He was still thinking about this wonderful statement when he heard a second song, "Every day, here or there, the wise little boy will always take care.'' Finally, there was this song, "No matter what you say, no matter what you do, always say 'I love you.'''

"O grandpa,'' he cried "I had the most wonderful dream. The Sukkah talked to me. Beautiful voices came through these boards and told me three things.'' Excitedly he shared with his grandfather the three little rhymes that he had heard. His grandfather started to explain them to him. "Thank you,'' he said, "is more than a spoken expression. It is a way of behaving. You not only say 'thank you,' you express your gratitude by doing nice things, by sharing with others the blessings God gives you. Tonight at your temple you will make offerings of fruits and vegetables. You will bring a little basket filled with lovely things to be sent to homes and hospitals, so that the people who are sick, and especially the children, will be able to share with you some of God's bounty. Isn't this the right way to express your thanks, by sharing?"

"But, Grandpa," he asked, "what about 'take care'?" His grandfather told him about the need to be careful, about the danger of driving an automobile too fast or being reckless. He told him about the accidents that can happen when people are not careful in their behavior. He said, "We have to remember that God wants us to take care of ourselves and others and always to be considerate of them." Suddenly Jimmy remembered that one of his classmates was in the hospital. He had been hurt in an accident caused by someone's carelessness.

Then his grandfather spoke about the words, "I love you." "Jimmy," he said, "if you love people and I hope you love many of them, tell them so! Put your arms around them and tell them that you love them. How happy this will always make your mother and father, your brothers and sisters, your grandma and grandpa. It is a way of making them feel that you have really become the kind of boy they want you to be, loving and thoughtful."

Jimmy moved quickly. He put his arms around his

grandfather and whispered, "I really love you, grandpa, and I promise that I will always remember what the Sukkah told me in my dream and what you told me today." So when little Jimmy came to Temple and saw the beautiful Sukkah, placed on the altar, he listened to the service and during the music he kept saying to himself, "I will never forget, those wonderful thoughts "Thank you," "Take care," and "I love you." And to the best of my knowledge, our friend Jimmy, who may be here at our service today, never forgot.

Rabbi Abraham Shusterman

* * *

Hidden Weapon

It happened on Rosh Hashanah, during the dark and grim days of the Nazi persecution. Although life was hard for the Jews of Germany, they still assembled in their synagogues, as in happier times, to pray to God that the old year and its afflictions be ended and the new year and its blessings begin. One of the largest synagogues in Berlin was filled to capacity. The service that year was especially solemn because of the shadow which hung over the Jews. Suddenly, above the sound of the prayers, the people heard with bated breath the sound of marching feet in the distance. A Nazi patrol

84

could bode no good. To the great alarm of the worshippers the patrol stopped outside the door of the synagogue. The door was flung open by an arrogant officer who bellowed: "We have received information that you are using this building to store secret weapons. We will conduct a search and until it is completed there will be no services." Then he ordered the patrol to search the entire building from top to bottom. After they had ransacked the synagogue, the storm troopers reported that no secret weapons were to be found. Just as they were about to leave, the eyes of the officer alighted upon the ark. "Aha," he exclaimed, "this must be the hiding place," and he strode to the ark and disdainfully swept the curtain open. But, to his chagrin, all that he found were the Torah Scrolls. Stepping forward the rabbi of the congregation said: "Yes, you are correct. The Torah is the secret weapon of the Jewish people. For it has sustained and preserved us through the ages. Its truths have been our sword and our armor against those who have sought to destroy us."

How true are the words of the rabbi! For whatever the conditions and the circumstances of his life, the Jew was spirtually preserved by the teachings of his Torah. It gave him life and strength in days of darkness. No wonder he thanked God for giving it to his forefathers. For without the Torah the Jew is like a body without a soul. It is the reason for his existence. It was his secret weapon in the past. And, if he studies and obeys it, it is his hope for the future. So if the Jew is to survive, his life must be centered in Torah, interpreted to meet the demands of modern life. It is not far-fetched to say that modern man will not survive the nuclear age unless he practices the Torah teachings of justice and righteousness, love and mercy. But the Jew has a special responsibility to be the guardian, the champion of the Torah, for it is the Jew to whom it first was given. It is the Jew who has preserved it through the centuries as it has preserved him.

In the words of the prayerbook: "It is a tree of life to them that hold fast to it and its supporters are happy. Its way are ways of pleasantness and all of its paths are peace."

Rabbi Albert A. Gordon

* * *

Give Thanks

At every major festival we Jews read and sing the beautiful 118th Psalm that opens and closes with the words, "Hodu ladoneye ki tov," "O give thanks unto the Lord for He is Good." Some of us know several melodies for that response. In another great psalm we are told, "It is good to give thanks unto the Lord, to sing praise to Thy name, O Most High."

The Hebrew language has almost magical powers. It often reveals the hidden. When you look closely, there suddenly appears a light. The word for "thanks" is a good example. We are never told to be or to feel grateful, but to give thanks, show gratitude. The true feeling of thankfulness is something you have only when you give it away! That is why our parents try so hard to teach us to say the magic words "Thank you!"

Who in the Bible is given credit for teaching us this important lesson? It is David, the shepherd who learned to play the harp, to compose songs, to help others through his music, and who later led his people against their enemies, the Philistines.

As a young boy David took care of the goats and lambs entrusted to him. He fed the lambkins the tenderest grass, and if a wild animal threatened his flock he would risk his own life to protect the helpless creatures. Seeing how faithful he was, God seemed to say, "David knows how to tend sheep, therefore he will be a good shepherd for my flock, the Children of Israel."

But we, too, can use our imagination and can picture the boy David in the pastureland. This is what might have happened.

One day he heard that a great bear had been sighted in the neighborhood. Suddenly he heard a sound that made him put down his harp. It was a long, shrill wail. David stood up and strained his eyes to peer into the darkness of the nearby forest. He entered the woods and came upon a clearing between tall trees where a trap had been dug. A huge bear had fallen into the trap, and it was he who was howling. At first, David had in mind to pick up a heavy tree-branch and finish off the bear in its fallen misery.

Suddenly the bear spoke words he could understand. "Help me, David," the bear was whimpering. "Save me, and I will forever stand guard for you and the other shepherds to drive away any animal that plans to attack you flocks." David found himself saying, "You will do that for me, just if I let you live?" And he heard the sound of the bear's cry melting into these words, "Yes, you will see. One act of kindness on your part, and I will show you a lifetime of thankfulness."

David set the bear free. The bear licked his hand and disappeared into the forest. David returned to watch his flocks at the edge of the woods. Often in the years that followed David would think about that strange episode. He strummed on his harp and said, "How wondrous are Thy works, O Lord! Even Thy wildest creatures can express their gratitude. How much more must we, Thy children, say, 'Give thanks unto the Lord for He is good, for His mercy endureth forever!'"

Rabbi Stanley R. Brav

.* * *

A Game of Checkers

It is told that Rabbi Nahum, the son of the Rabbi of Rishyn, entered the House of Study at a time when he was not expected, and found his disciples playing checkers. When they saw their beloved teacher they were embarrassed and stopped playing. But he nodded to them kindly and asked: "Do you know the rules of the game of checkers?" And when they did not reply out of shame, the teacher proceeded to explain: "I shall explain the game to you. The first rule is that one must not make two moves at once. The second is that one may only move forward and not backward. And the third is that when one has reached the last row, one may move wherever one likes."

A popular and ancient game may provide us with a key to life. The first rule of the game of checkers is that we must not make two moves at once.

People sometimes become so awed by the thought of everything that has to be done in life that they don't do anything. I have known young people who, in a rush for popularity, must join everything, participate in everything, waste away hundreds of hours to be a part of everything. The result is that they are really a part of nothing. Some of our college people are in such a constant state of bewilderment about their careers and ideals, that they flounder for want of a goal.

In the religious realm the late Dr. Leo Baeck was once asked, "How can a Jew live as a Jew under modern conditions?" He replied, "I always advise, begin with not too many things, take one step at a time."

The second rule in checkers is that we must move forward and not backward.

To all people the Psalmist speaks about lifting one's

eyes to the mountains. In essence he tells us to have high goals. Judaism speaks of that which shall be, the future. "Tell the children of Israel that they move forward," was the charge to the Israelites before the Red Sea. In every phase of life our sights must be raised to noble ideals. Standing still really means moving backward. Judaism offers us the opportunity to say, "How glorious are Thy works, O Lord." The possibilities for growth are always before us.

The third rule of checkers is that when we have reached our goal, we may move in any direction.

Once we have accomplished our aims in life, we can begin to move about. To save the world one must save himself and must fortify himself with goals and visions. Later one can afford the joy which comes from devoting one's talents toward the betterment of mankind.

The tragedy of our time is that so many talented and capable people, after attaining important ends, do not seek to contribute to other objectives. The two go hand in hand and our religion speaks to us to "do justly, love mercy and walk humbly with our God."

Life's course can be purposeful if we make one move at a time, if we move forward and not backward, and when after taking hold of our personal problems, we move ahead to do God's work on earth.

Rabbi Alvan D. Rubin

* * *

The Answer Is in Your Hands

Many years ago there lived a wise and learned man by the name of Maimonides. Maimonides was not only a scholar but also a physician. And as one of the most famous physicians of his day he was asked to take care of the royal family.

The king's physicians did not like the thought of an intruder caring for the king and taking their place. So they devised a test to prove to the king that Maimonides was not worthy of being his personal physician.

The test was for one of the men to hold a little bird in his closed hand and ask Maimonides whether the bird was alive. But unknown to the king and to Maimonides the test was so arranged that Maimonides could not possibly hope to pass it. For if Maimonides said the bird was alive, this cruel man was going to crush it. And if Maimonides said that the bird was not alive, then the man would open his hand and let the bird fly away.

The time for the test came, and all were gathered to see whether Maimonides was as wise as some people thought. Then, when Maimonides was asked the question he turned to the man holding the bird and said, "The answer is in your hands."

And this is what we must tell ourselves. The answer is in our hands to decide whether or not we are going to live worthwhile lives and be worthwhile people. It is for us to decide whether we are going to spend our time well or waste it, devote ourselves to worthy causes or be selfish and uninterested.

Rabbi Irwin M. Blank

* * *

Your Tree of Life

In a perceptive parable, the Midrash relates how once a bird nestled on a branch. As the bird glided gracefully through the heavenly environs, the branch was filled with chagrin and envy, for it looked upon itself as being imprisoned to the trunk of the tree and it wistfully longed for the freedom and unshackled mobility of the bird.

Pleadingly and poignantly the branch turned heavenward and prayed to God that He in His mercy would liberate it from the trunk so that it could enjoy the zest of unbridled freedom personified by the winging bird gliding through the sky gracefully and gleefully.

The Midrashic parable continues that God hearkened unto the prayer of the branch by sending a mighty gale wrenching the branch from its rootage to the trunk, lifting it heavenward. As the branch soared upward, a lilting song of freedom reverberated through its being. It was blissful in the awareness that now it had the birdlike

quality of zestfully gliding through the serene elements.
After a few hours, however, the gale subsided, hurling the branch into a gutter and setting into motion the slow but inevitable process of decay. Shorn now of its source of nourishment, the branch began to dry up and rot until finally what was formerly a beautiful twig pulsating with life-energy coursing through its petals was now reduced to an ashen heap of debris and rubbish.

Prior to its expiration, the branch realized the foolishness of its original longing. In the moment of agony, it understood fully that the rootage to the trunk was not a sraight-jacket, stifling and repressing, but was rather the very artery of its life pouring into the branch the sap of sustenance, invigorating it to grow and luxuriate in all of God's glory.

In a penitential and confessional mood, it now turned to God asking for forgiveness in its realization that what it had deemed as a rigid, stricturing burden was verily its fount of life.

Our Torah heritage has been likened by the prophets unto a tree. The Torah is termed Etz Chaim, Tree of Life. Every family represents a branch on this majestic and glorious Tree, with each individual Jew being a leaf on the branch of the Tree of Life which is Judaism. Too often in our estrangement from Jewish life and our alienation from Jewish values, we, as the branch, foolishly look upon our Torah heritage and synagogue affiliation as being a straight-jacket, stifling us and onerously repressing us. Too often we echo the words of Heine, that Judaism is not a religion but a catastrophe.

Some Jews seek to be liberated from their spiritual rootage in the quest for a birdlike type of freedom. Alas, through bitter experiences, many learn that the trunk which was looked upon with contempt was indeed the source of one's life. To be an alienated Jew shorn from faith in God, Torah, and the mission of the peoplehood of Israel, is indeed a tragic experience not only for the Jewish people but for one's personal life. Rollo May, a profound student of human nature, speaking from a vast psychoanalytical background, states that the curse of modern man is the emptiness in his inner being. Modern man has filled his soul with the rubbish of sawdust, like the insides of a cheap doll.

Modern man, living in an age of so-called affluence, laden with an abundance of gadgets, has learned anew the profound truth of the words, "Man does not live by bread alone." It is not enough merely to nourish the body as we allow the mind and soul to suffer from starvation. This malnutritious diet has created what is called "The Hollow Generation." Even as nature abhors a vacuum so does human nature abhor a vacuum of mind and soul. It is this emptiness which is the source of man's misery.

Blessed were our forefathers who every morning upon rising turned heavenward and in gratitude recited the words:

> Happy are we!
> How goodly our portion!
> How blessed our lot!
> How beautiful our heritage!

There is a story that Queen Victoria said to Disraeli, "You were born into the Jewish faith but through your father you renounced Judaism. But you do not practice the rites of the church nor conform to its traditions. What are you?" Wistfully came the reply. "Your Majesty, I am the empty page between the Old and the New Testament."

To be an empty page is probably the most abysmal tragedy that a person can experience, for estrangement deprives life of meaning.

Only by grafting your life into the Etz Chaim, the Tree of Life of religious commitment, will you derive from its trunk the nourishment for your mind and soul. Instead of being a cipher let us write a luminous chapter adding to the glory of a 4,000 year old Torah Tradition, spun by patriarchs, prophets, saints, scholars, and students.

Once a culprit was brought before Alexander the Great, the world conqueror, who upon hearing the evidence leveled against the accused, condemned him to death as a criminal. The defendant knew he was innocent. In a quavering voice, he turned to the implacable ruler stating, "Your Majesty, I appeal this verdict." Upon hearing these unexpected words the mighty ruler turned to the doomed creature and proudly said, "Appeal! appeal to whom? Don't you know that I am the final authority and that beyond me there is no recourse?" The condemned man listened to these arrogant words, straightened his back and with dignity uttered the challenging words, "Your Majesty, I appeal from Alexander the *small* to Alexander the *Great*."

In every person there lives a great self and a small self. Blessed will be the day when you, through the blueprint of our spiritual heritage, will be able to effect the grand transformation of sublimating your small unto your great.

Rabbi Louis L. Sacks

* * *

Not To Be Sinful

In the Ethics of the Fathers, a section of the Talmud, there is a brief phrase of the most lofty significance. The book is full of priceless counsel. But this verse is of special significance to anyone troubled by the problem of human evil.

Averah goreret averah, "One transgression brings another in its train." Once a sin has been committed, conscience becomes dulled, and it is easy to repeat the wrong act.

For many years at the Penitentiary of the City of New York(now also known as the Correctional Institution for Men), Jewish inmates never made up more than 2 percent of the total. And strangely enough, the persons most proud of this record have been the Jewish prisoners themselves, even though they are behind bars for their misdeeds.

When my older son was sixteen I took him with me to the prison to watch the inmates at their Friday service. After we had visited the hospital and offices and seen the cell blocks, we joined the congregation in the chapel. An inmate volunteered to lead the brief service. The chaplain spoke briefly. Reading matter was handed out, and then there was time for fraternization.

I noted a group of inmates clustered about my son, all speaking with deep earnestness. When they had returned to their cells, he related the gist of their conversation.

"You're a boy yet," they had said, "and we can give you advice, even though they call us 'bad' and we're locked up. Just one thing, never start doing anything wrong; because after the first time you are likely to do it again. Then you'll have the habit, and you may end up here."

Then one had pointed to me.

"There's your father. He never started sinning, so he became a rabbi. He goes home from here, and we stay on. Be like him!"

I was of course pleased by the faith in me expressed in the compliment, but I was more impressed by the application of the teaching of the Talmud. As I thought over the individual life stories confided to me by the inmates, I found the same pattern in every one.

> The first time I went out with this fellow, I knew he was no good, but I kept on running around with him and some of his friends, until we all landed here. My brother told me to stay away from the guy, and I didn't listen. They dared me to bare my arm and try the needle. I

97

felt I shouldn't do it, but I gave in, and after awhile I was hooked. I hope this prison term will cure me of the dope habit, but I see the same junkie coming back all the time.

I was working in this department store, and they made me a salesman of electric razors. I had the impulse one day, and slipped a razor into my pocket. No one noticed what I did, nor did anyone see the bulge in my pocket. I felt pretty cheap and guilty when I went out for the day. I hid the razor in a drawer. The next week something seemed to push me into repeating the theft. When half a dozen razors had disappeared, someone must have grown suspicious. Detectives came to my house. They knew just where to look. My mother screamed when they pulled me away.

I used to hold my temper in, but one day I got mad over nothing and hit a fellow so hard his head struck the pavement and he passed out. I ran away. But no one came after me to arrest me. I got into all kinds of fights; I was winning them all. What happened to get me sentenced? I'm married now, and one day in an argument I knocked my wife unconscious.

Thus the stories went. Always the first time, and the final appearance before the judge. One sin followed inevitably upon another.

Remember that this is the major purpose of your religious studies and services, to keep you from taking the first step that may lead to your destruction. A Jew who attends his religious school, who observes the ethical and religious commandments of his faith, who never forgets or neglects the teachings of our sages, will never find himself locked out from society, despised and shunned by those who know of his evil record. Even when a sinner has turned completely away from his wicked ways; there are too many who refuse any longer to trust him. But worst of all, often the sinner is afraid to trust himself.

Learn what Judaism has to tell you. Emulate your forefathers, your teachers, and religious leaders, and you will find it a simple matter to resist the first temptation to do wrong, a first that may bring a hundred evil acts in its train.

Rabbi Abraham Burstein

* * *

Praying to God

Our prayers do not have to be long and eloquent for God to hear them. The sincere prayer is the beautiful prayer. There is a story in the Talmud which illustrates this simple truth. One of Rabbi Eleazar's students was reading the Sabbath Service at a leisurely pace. His fellow students complained about this: "How he drags out the prayers!" Then Rabbi Eleazar responded to this complaint: "Does he pray any longer than Moses, our teacher, whose devotion on Mount Sinai lasted forty days and forty nights?" Sometime later another student was officiating at prayer and he, on the contrary, raced through the service like a whirlwind. His fellow students complained: "How fast he reads the prayers!" And then Rabbi Eleazar responded to this: "Is his praying briefer than that of Moses, our teacher, when he prayed for the recovery of his sister Miriam with the words: 'Heal her, O God!'?"

We cannot judge a prayer to be "good" or "bad" by its length or the rate of speed it is recited. The right prayer comes from the heart whether it is said in forty days or in a few seconds. Perhaps you have heard the story of the simple shepherd boy who could not read or write, but who could play the flute beautifully. His melodies were admired by all the people in the surrounding villages.

One year, when the High Holydays came around, the shepherd boy decided that he would go to the nearest synagogue to pray. It just so happened that the nearest synagogue was very famous because the Baal Shem Tov, the great Hasidic teacher, prayed there. The little boy entered the synagogue on Rosh Hashanah. As he quietly sat down he was suddenly troubled because he couldn't read the prayers. He realized that he had never been taught to pray! But he loved God and always thought about Him. Then he thought that perhaps God would appreciate it if he expressed himself in the best way he knew.

And so, in the midst of the solemn assembly of worshippers, the shepherd boy took out his flute and began to play a beautiful melody. A hush fell over the assembly. The worshippers stopped their prayers shocked by this interruption. One man stood up and shouted: "Get him out of the synagogue!" Another arose from his seat, and still another. Eventually all the men were standing and shouting.

The little boy was frightened, and as he was about to run away he felt a hand gently rest upon his shoulder. He looked up and beheld the Baal Shem Tov looking into his scared eyes, a calm smile upon his lips. When the rest of the men saw this, they ceased their shouting. The synagogue was completely quiet.

Then the Baal Shem Tov spoke softly. "This small boy has prayed in the most sincere way that he knows. God will surely hear his prayer. God will hear."

We need not resort to playing musical instruments when we want to pray to God. But neither do we have to grope for the right words. We don't have to feel that every prayer we utter must be a Shakesperean soliloquy. As long as we are sincere in our desire to communicate with God, as long as our prayers are deeply and honestly felt, we will benefit.

Rabbi Jack D. Spiro

* * *

Which Way?

Occasionally, indignant parents and students express themselves as follows: "It isn't fair, it isn't right; there is too much dishonesty during examinations, attendance in class, and at services." Now, this indictment may be extreme but there are times when it is altogether true. There has been cheating during tests, especially during the Confirmation Comprehensive Review. There has been dishonesty when our youngsters were to report for the Friday afternoon lectures, when they were to sign in for Vespers and report for Family Worship. We recognize the problem and then take certain measures. But what about you, you students who see this? In what direction should you turn? What should you do?

The most obvious reaction is to become resentful and state that if others are dishonest, why should we be concerned? We too, will take the easy way out and settle down to a comfortable existence with little or no strain on our part. What is most painful in this regard is the temptation to fall in with those who are as indifferent as we, to associate with those who "couldn't care less" or, what is worse, to dwell amongst those who want to be graduated but who are bereft of any sense of morality. Thus, the easy way can become the immoral way.

When we proceed in this fashion, we become like Lot in the Bible: Lot separated from Abraham, and in so doing, he chose "the plain of the Jordan," a rich, luxurious land. This spot gave the promise, the rabbis tell us, of an easy, untroubled existence where there would be no hardship or problems. But, in his desire for comfort, Lot was not careful and he moved amongst the people of Sodom who "were wicked and sinners against the Lord exceedingly." Thus, he dwelled in the midst of people who were the prototype of all that is degrading. When one reacts in this fashion he is either influenced for evil or, at the very least, he amounts to nothing. He does not count and history passes him by.

The late historian, Arnold Toynbee, told us that when the early settlers came to America they found New England to be the least likely place in which to thrive and be productive. New England is a barren, bleak, and harsh land. Yet, as Toynbee pointed out, New England, particularly Massachusetts, has meant so much to the United States. It has been one of our most famous areas in terms of accomplishment. This example and others moved Toynbee to observe that great difficulties, even hardships, can and do stimulate many people. He told us that what we need is a challenge to which we can respond. As a matter of fact, this famous historian has become quite well known by the phrase, "challenge and response"—frequently, when there is no challenge, there is little or no response to life and we do not amount to much.

Perhaps Abraham, unlike Lot, understood this. In separating from Lot he selected "the land of Canaan" which is characterized by difficult topography. It is either a hard and rocky soil or a place given to marshes. As such, it is completely different from the rich area, "the cities of the Plain" alongside Sodom where Lot dwelled. In other words, Abraham kept himself far from the ease and comfort which appealed to his nephew, keeping himself apart from the corrupting influence of Sodom. Abraham struck out to a place that would challenge his creative and spiritual potential.

Somewhere along life's highway we all have to face the choice Abraham faced. Do we settle down like Lot to an untroubled existence, unconcerned and refusing to be disturbed, taking our Jewishness in a nonchalant fashion, all the while associating with those who react in a similar manner? Or are we like Abraham, willing to respond to the challenge placed before us? Do we have the strength of character not to accede to the easy path nor associate with those who do, lest they pull us down to their level? Ours should be the resolve to choose the hard way, to wrestle, grope and struggle as we seek to comprehend what it means to be a Jew. It is time to ask: How can I learn what is expected of me as one who is born into the covenant of Abraham our father?

People who lack the inner fortitude of an Abraham make no contribution to society. Life passes them by and we never hear of them. They exist by going through the motions but they do not truly live. When we have the determination of an Abraham we may be assured that our character will become enriched and that we will make our mark upon the society in which we live as we fulfill the Scriptural admonition, "in Thee shall all the families of the earth be blessed."

Rabbi Frederick C. Schwartz

* * *

104

The Meaning of the Symbols of Adam and the Garden of Eden

No lesson on human nature is more illuminating than the one presented through the symbols of Adam and the Garden of Eden. According to the Scriptural narrative, Adam is placed in the Garden of Eden. He is provided with every conceivable human need. He is even promised everlasting life. Except for one simple test which he is expected to meet, there is nothing left for him to wish for. The test was not to partake of the fruit from one special tree. "And the Lord God commanded the man saying: Of every tree of the Garden you are free to eat; but as for the tree of knowledge of good and bad you must not eat of it, for as soon as you eat of it, you shall be doomed to die." This certainly was not asking too much from Adam in return for all that he was given. It would appear then that he would make every effort to pass this simple test with flying colors. After all, why would he want to forfeit a life of ease, and especially the promise of eternal life, for so small a sacrifice? But, contrary to our expectations, Adam permits temptation to gain the upper hand. He eats from the forbidden fruit. He fails the test. As a punishment, he is driven from the Garden. From this point on, Adam's life is never the same.

His eyes are opened to a new world. He learns to know right and wrong, good and evil, sorrow and joy, tears and laughter, defeat and victory, hope and disappointment, frustration and self-fulfillment. He must now toil to get all the things previously taken care of for him in the Garden. "By the sweat of your brow shall you get bread to eat, until you return to the ground, for from it you were taken; for dust you are and to dust shall you return" (Gen. 3:19).

Adam's days in the Garden never varied. Each day was a repetition of the previous one. In our world, days are unpredictable. We never know what the morrow has in store for us. One day the reward for one's labors is peace and contentment. The next day the compensation may be sadness and tension. So man struggles for the few years to which his eternal life has been reduced until he is claimed by eternal death.

Using the symbols of Adam and the Garden (Paradise), what lesson does this narrative seek to convey? The author subtly tries to impress upon us the lesson that human nature cannot be satisfied with Paradise; that human nature requires worlds to conquer, mysteries to unlock, high mountain peaks to reach, visions to be inspired by, goals to work for, and causes to be dedicated to. Paradise, according to the author, is discovered not in things done but things to be done; not in missions performed but in missions to be performed; not in the attainment of an ideal but in the pursuit of it. He tries to show that Adam, man, is not happy when he achieves Paradise. He prefers hard work to idleness. He accepts pain, which is the price of knowledge, instead of bliss which is the promise of ignorance. He chooses the curse of a brief life ending in death, rather than a useless, colorless, one. He values the pleasure of giving far above that of receiving. He is happier with the thought that Paradise is beckoning to him from a distance, than with the feeling of having achieved it.

In short, the author would have us believe that Paradise lost is Paradise regained; that imagining it is more exciting and more rewarding than experiencing it.

Rabbi Samuel Umen

*   *   *

Molasses versus Vinegar

Once upon a time, when horses and wagons still shared the use of our streets, little Sam, ten years old, was walking on Broadway in New York City. When he came to the intersection of 42nd Street and Broadway, he saw a huge crowd standing around a horse and wagon. The wagon was a big one, standing just at the crossroads. The horse had slipped on the ice and was lying on the ground.

The teamster and two policemen, together with some bystanders, tried to get the horse to rise. They beat him, pulled his reins, prodded him, kicked him, pleaded with him and yelled. But the horse lay stolidly upon the ground and would not budge an inch.

Sam watched for about ten minutes and then went over to the policeman and said, "I know how you can get the horse up." At first the policeman did not even notice the little boy, but when Sam insisted, the policeman finally yelled, "Get out of here, you scamp! Let me alone. Here are grown, experienced men who cannot get the horse to stand up and you think you can do it. Now, get out!"

Sam waited a few more minutes and then, without asking anyone, and unnoticed by the policeman, went over to the horse. He stuck his hand in his pocket and pulled out a lump of sugar. He put his hand with the sugar in it near the nostrils of the horse. The horse, smelling the sugar, stretched out his neck in order to take it into his mouth, but the boy pulled his hand away. He then kept his hand close to the mouth and nose of the horse, always pulling it away as the horse reached for it. Gradually the horse stretched his neck as far as it could go, then began to lift his forelegs and then his hind legs, and then stood up, and as Sam led the horse over to the sidewalk, he allowed the horse to take the lump of sugar into its mouth. He had accomplished his aim, and all the people stood about amazed at the boy's innate wisdom.

So, you see that very often shouting and yelling, becoming annoyed and angry and impatient will not bring about the results you look for. It is true that you can catch more flies with molasses than you can with vinegar. A warm smile, a soft word, a gentle plea, the use of good judgment, any one or all of these will more often than not bring reward to your efforts and accomplishment of your desired goals and aims.

Rabbi Louis Parris

* * *

The Rabbi's Anguish

Several hundred years ago there lived a great Rabbi in the city of Berdichov in the southwestern part of Russia. His name was Levi Yitzchok.

This Rabbi had a large synagogue, and Jews from all over the world came to pray and worship with him. There were very few chairs in the synagogue, so most worshippers would stand throughout the service.

Into this synagogue one bright morning little Sam wandered, and watched with great interest and fascination what was going on. He saw the Rabbi standing near the Ark, completely covered by his huge tallit bending in every direction, swaying backward and forward and sidewards, from time to time lifting his head and arms to heaven as if pleading with God, and gesticulating violently as he raised his voice in prayer.

Sam waited until the end of the service, and he noticed after the Rabbi doffed his tallit, that it was completely wet from perspiration, as were the Rabbi's clothes. He wondered why, but did not have the courage to ask.

That evening Sam saw the Rabbi going through the same violent motions as he stood in prayer. The next day he returned to the synagogue and in great wonderment he again witnessed, with mouth agape and wide-open eyes, the same scene. As he watched the Rabbi, he noticed another worshipper in the far end of the synagogue standing near the rostrum going through the same motions. Sam saw the sexton walk over to the young man and say to him, "Young man, they will surely kill you!" At this time the young man looked up, and asked why. The sexton walked away saying, "You will see."

Later Sam saw the same sexton walk over to the young man and heard the same conversation repeated. This happened a third and fourth and fifth time at subsequent services. After the sixth time, the young man walked over to the sexton at the conclusion of the service and asked, "Why do you come to me with such a sinister message that I will be killed? Have I done anything wrong?"

The sexton answered, "My son, you are imitating the Rabbi in his movements and gesticulations."

"Is it a crime to follow in the footsteps of the Rabbi?" asked the young man.

"No," replied the sexton. "There is much that you can learn from the Rabbi and it is good to follow in his footsteps, but you must first prove yourself worthy and have the same sincerity and deep faith that he possesses. Until you achieve these, you simply observe, study and learn his piety and wisdom."

The young man shook his head and said, "I cannot understand what you mean."

Whereupon, the sexton told him a story:

Once a farmer had a rooster and many hens. The rooster would crow loudly at the crack of dawn and thus would wake up the farmer and his family. The farmer's wife would bring some milk and food to the rooster and then proceed to do her chores.

The hens, noticing this, became jealous, and one

bright hen said one day, "I can't understand this. Here we are giving the farmer the eggs that he wants and serving him to the best of our ability, and yet we are not treated with any special kindness or favor. This rooster, who never laid an egg in his life, and who is lazy and shiftless, all he has to do is to raise his voice and crow in the morning and he is given special food and attention. This is an unfair world and I am going to do something to correct it! Tomorrow morning I am going to crow, and I will receive the reward that I deserve."

Next morning this hen did crow. Once, twice, three times,loudly. The farmer's wife, hearing this, ran out to the barn with an axe and grabbed the hen that crowed, and was just about to chop its head off when the hen turned to the farmer's wife and pitifully asked, "Why do you do this to me? What have I done?"

"You have crowed.Don't you know that when a hen crows bad luck will come to the farmer's household unless the hen is instantly killed?"

"But the rooster crows and you reward him, and when I crow you kill me!"

"Ah," said the farmer's wife,"you don't understand. The reason the rooster crows is because at the crack of dawn an angel from heaven comes down and scorches the rooster under his wings with red-hot irons. He crows because it hurts him; he is being scorched. Has the angel touched you with any red-hot tongs that you must crow?"

As the sexton concluded the story, the young man looked up at him and said, "I have truly learned a wonderful lesson today. You mean to say that the Rabbi is all heart, and his heart aches for all humanity. The suffering of mankind consumes his very soul, and that is why he sways back and forth so violently and gesticulates and lifts his head and arms in prayer, pleading for humanity and for God's mercy."

"That's right," answered the sexton. "You must study and learn and live a pious good life, and some day you too may feel, even in a small degree, his anguish. At that time you, too, will be impelled to emulate the Rabbi."

Rabbi Louis Parris

* * *

Two Types of Discontentment

There are two types of discontentment among human beings. One type is negative, destructive, a curse to its possessor and all around him. The other type is of a positive nature, is constructive, a blessing to the possessor. The one who suffers from the negative type of discontentment is a person who lacks faith in God, in himself, and in his fellow man. He regards his life as a failure and blames society for it. He is bitter, depressed, self-centered, lonely and melancholy. He views the world without plan and without purpose. He sees no value in anything. His only contribution to the world is his moan. "Vanity of vanities, all is vanity," the opening verse of Ecclesiastes, briefly sums up the life of this sick soul.

The healthy-minded person also suffers from discontentment. His discontentment leads to action. All the progress in the world is the result of his impatience. Always dissatisfied with things as they are, he constantly works to make the world a better place to live in, and man's lot on earth a happier one. Through science, he seeks to make life easier. Through medicine, he discovers cures for many dreaded diseases. Through politics and government, he aims to increase justice, freedom, security and peace. Through religion, he endeavors to enrich the spirit, instill righteousness and love. Through art, music and literature, he aims to cultivate an appreciation for beauty and harmony, and to inspire thought.

He sees life as a task continuously demanding his efforts, talents and ability, to build and rebuild, create and recreate. For nothing is perfect and everything can be improved. Sensing the world's need for him, it is to the world's work that he gives himself. He does what he is able to do best, and whatever he undertakes to do, he does with his whole heart and soul.

If "Vanity of vanities, all is vanity," the opening verse of Ecclesiastes, is the cry of the useless life, the life without hope and faith, the sick soul, then one of the closing verses of the same book, "Fear the Lord and keep His commandments for this is the whole man," is the counsel and advice of the healthy-minded person

113

who by his discontentment enriches the world and gives meaning and purpose to life.

Rabbi Samuel Umen

* * *

4-H Club

When the Syrian military camp laid siege to the capital city of Israel, the inhabitants were faced with starvation. Food could not be bought for any price. King Jehoram apparently charged the prophet Elisha with responsibility for the unbearable situation, suggesting that the prophet encouraged the people to maintain their desperate resistance under siege.

Elisha took up the king's challenge. He predicted that the siege would be lifted and that within twenty-four hours an abundance of food would flood the market. The king's officer who heard the prediction scoffed: "Even if the Lord should make windows in heaven, can such a thing happen?"

It did happen. The miracle came to pass, as the prophet foretold. The Syrian camp was suddenly frightened by an uncanny midnight disturbance. Thinking that the king of Israel had hired a foreign army to overwhelm them, the Syrians fled helter-skelter, leaving behind them their huge stocks of provisions. The

114

next day, the inhabitants of Samaria were amazed to learn that the siege had been lifted overnight. They rushed out of their beleaguered city and came upon stores of food left by the retreating enemy. The miracle did happen. God did make windows in heaven.

Let us get to the heart of this miracle. Who discovered that the Syrian army had fled overnight? Was it the king's officer, or his scouts? That would have been in line of duty. But it did not happen that way. It was a group of lepers who came upon the abandoned camp, and reported the good news. They said, "This is a day of good tidings, shall we keep it quiet?"

Outcasts became the bearers of good tidings. This was a miracle!

History knows many incidents which reveal the miraculous in human experience. Let us recall one such "unbelievable" event in American history.

> When the Pilgrim Fathers at last dropped anchor in Plymouth Harbor, the prospect of the bare December woods must have made many a heart sink in secret. . . . Fortunately, the kind providence in which they so firmly believed had led them to the site of an abandoned Indian village. . . . So it turned out that the Pilgrims found land already cleared for them, as well as a hidden store of grain that carried them through the first grim winter. (*Changing Face of New England*, by Betty Fanders Thompson.) American history opened with windows in heaven.

Indeed, God has ways of working wonders beyond human grasp. He sometimes makes the handicapped bearers of good tidings, and the helpless messengers of comfort. God has it in His power to turn a Helen Keller, who from infancy was condemned to sit outside the gate of human communication, into a messenger of salvation and a source of inspiration to those confined in the prison of blindness. Wherever she went, she lifted the siege of human isolation, and was the messenger of life and hope. One of God's windows in heaven. Let Helen Keller speak for herself, "I thank God for my handicaps, for through them I have found myself, my work and my God."

God opens windows in heaven. A paralyzed Roosevelt, apparently doomed to spend his remaining years in a wheelchair, away from political life, became the bearer of good tidings to a world besieged by totalitarian powers. The man who was helpless without his crutches crossed oceans to help bring relief to a beleaguered humanity.

Desperation leads to daring, the first step in the direction of the miraculous. There is no guarantee that daring will always be rewarded, yet when it happens we are witnesses to a miracle, that of discovery. The desperation of the lepers which led to their daring move ended in discovery, the finding of abundant stores of food in the abandoned camp. That discovery meant deliverance for a besieged city.

When three-year-old Louis Braille was boring holes with an awl in a heavy piece of leather in his father's harness shop, an accident with the awl caused blindness. That was in France, in the year 1812. Seventeen years later the totally blind youth invented the Braille system, a system now used all over the world, enabling

116

the blind to enjoy the treasures of literature.

If one were to trace the saga of medicine, especially of modern miracle drugs, he would come upon the same process: daring born of desperation leading to deliverance through discovery. Indeed, many significant human achievements as well as great discoveries which resulted in the improvement of human life had their beginnings in situations bordering despair. In all instances there were those who, like the king's officer, mocked the prophets of a better tomorrow. Yet, people of vision proved that God does make windows in heaven, to help one person bring deliverance to humanity to lift the siege of sickness, hunger, and fear. This is the miracle of the helpless!

Rabbi Solomon D. Goldfarb

* * *

Why Religious School?

"Why is it important to come to religious school?" I'll bet you ask that question every once in a while, particularly when it's a nice morning and you'd rather be playing ball or shopping. It's a question you ask of your parents, and a question you probably ask of yourselves, too. But have you ever had the nerve to ask

117

your rabbi? Well, if you haven't, let me ask it for you—and then let me try to answer.

Why is it important to go to religious school? It's important because religious school is a wonderful place to learn about *God*. Now I know you can learn about God in other places as well, but here in the synagogue, in God's house, we have the perfect atmosphere. We are among other Jewish boys and girls who have many of the same questions about God that we do, we have the synagogue library where we may read books about our history and our people and learn about God and His relationship to the Jewish people, and we have our teachers who can help us in our understanding. So, we come to religious school because it is a wonderful place to learn about God and then to put His teachings into practice in our daily lives.

It's also important to come to religious school because here we can learn and study about our *religion*. You know that ours is one of the oldest religions in the world, so there is lots to learn! We have an exciting history, a long literary tradition, and a very special way of life. If we are to be intelligent and well-informed Jews, and if we are to explain our religion to people of other faiths, then it is important for us to know as much about our religion as we can. What better place is there to learn than in religious school?

But this is only half the story. We ought to come to religious school to take advantage of the wonderful *opportunity* that is ours. Of course you know that there are boys and girls, just like yourselves, who live in countries where they aren't allowed to worship God.

118

They don't have the opportunity of religious expression, or of studying religious history. But here in America we are blessed with religious freedom, and may worship in the synagogue or church of our choice. "Proclaim liberty throughout the land unto all the inhabitants thereof," our Bible tells us. We can proclaim this liberty as often as we like, by enjoying the gift of religious freedom.

Finally, it is important to come to religious school because here we may gather in organized *worship* with our friends. Here we may utilize our prayer book to help us express our religious feelings, or we may create meaningful religious services of our own. Here is the place where our study assumes the form of worship, where our service to man is a way of worshipping God.

Four key words: God, Religion, Opportunity, and Worship.

Four important reasons why we should come to religious school. Look at these words for a minute. Do you see anything *else* in them? If you take the first letter of each word, you will see that they spell G-R-O-W. Thus, if you are concerned about God, religion, opportunity, and worship, you will understand why it is important to come to religious school, and you will *grow* as an American Jew.

Rabbi Richard J. Lehrman

* * *

119

The Other Apple

Everybody knows the story about the apple in the Garden of Eden. But did you know there was another apple? It is not mentioned in the Bible, but it is part of our tradition just the same.

It was a lovely summer day, perhaps too hot for a long walk. So the hiker looked around for a tree with many branches, and sat down in the shade for a rest. No one knows how long he sat there, nor whether he realized he was leaning against an apple tree.

What we *do* know is that an apple dropped off a twig, and bounced off this man's head! What's so wonderful about that, you ask? Well, many a person would have taken a bite of that juicy apple and walked off without another moment's thought. We would have been a little more rested, but that's about all; we would never have thought about it again.

But not the man in our story, not Isaac Newton in England around the year 1700. An idea struck him when that apple struck him. The force of that idea was much more important to the world than the apple itself.

Newton was the first man in the history of the world to tell us about gravity. As he rubbed his head he realized that everything falls down, not up, and this is gravity. Nowadays this seems so obvious that we can only wonder why it took mankind thousands of years to stumble upon it!

120

Perhaps after Newton realized this basic bit of science he *did* eat the apple. I would have, wouldn't you?

* * *

Miracles Do Happen

Miracles do happen and we ought to say "Thank You" to God for them.

Some of us may wish to give thanks for our wealth, and others for our health; some for our homes and others for our fine families. But these are only the results of the wonders which God has regularly performed for us.

What are these miracles? Is it that God split the Red Sea to let His children march from slavery to freedom? Is it that He made the sun and moon and stars stand still to give Joshua victory? Is it that He took Elijah from the earth in a fiery chariot to save His prophet the pain of death? Is it that He let Elisha bring a dead boy back to life to reward a mother's faith? These stories, probably mythical, deal with the suspension of natural law.

Should we give thanks for the marvels of modern science? Well, let us remember that these have become capable of killing as well as healing, of tearing down as well as building up. So we often fear them rather than praise them.

121

In our prayer book we read that God "does great things past finding out and miracles without number; He keeps us alive and does not suffer our foot to stumble." The very fact that we are alive is a most wondrous thing.

Our prayer book also calls us up to give thanks to the Ruler of the world "by Whose law the shadows of evening fall and the gates of night are opened." Thus we marvel at the light of day. In order that we might see, God sends light from the sun to the earth at a speed of 186,000 miles per second. In order that one side of the globe should not be baked while the other side freezes, He spins it around, once every twenty-four hours giving us, on the earth's surface, a ride at a speed of approximately 1,000 miles an hour. To give us the pleasant variety of changing seasons, He takes us for another trip, around the sun. To complete this trip once a year, we cover 1,600,000 miles per day at 67,000 miles per hour, three times as fast as our astronauts circling the globe.

Perhaps a miracle ought to be something spectacular, like water flowing uphill. God does just that for us when, in the words of the Psalmist, "He makes the clouds his chariot and walks upon the wings of the wind," every time it rains. Every glass of water we drink and every drop of water that irrigates our fields and groves was lifted out of the ocean by God's invisible pumping system. It was distilled on the way so it wouldn't be salty to the taste or poisonous to the soil. It was whisked through the air on the wings of a cloud and then dropped somewhere to come to our homes and gardens via river or lake and water pipe.

Perhaps we look for the dramatic miracle, that of the dead coming to life. We have that, too, in every grain of wheat that is plucked from a dead dry stalk, that is placed in the dark dead earth and that rises out of the grave, a living plant and a source of life for the children of man.

One recent morning, over the breakfast cereal, our six-year-old mused: "Daddy, we ought to thank God for making cows because they make milk for us." We grown-ups may think that by having our scientists observe and analyze the transformation of grass and roots and grain into a fatty, white liquid, we have a right to shrug it off as merely the result of biochemistry. All the processes of nature, which we so blithely take for granted, are they not all miraculous?

As we go through life, with all its problems and tribulations, with its disappointments and heartaches, we might well bear in mind this homely bit of advice:

I've been countin' up my blessin's, I've been summin' up my woes
But I ain't got the conclusions some would nat'rally suppose,
Why, I quit a-countin' troubles 'fore I had half a score
While the more I count my blessin's I keep findin' more and more!
There's been things that wa'n't exactly as I thought they'd ought to be,
An' I often growled at Providence for not a 'pettin' me,
But I hadn't stopped to reckon what the other side had been,

How much o' good an' blessin' had been thickly
  crowded in.
For there's been a gift o' sunshine after every shower o'
  tears,
An' a lot of consolation with every show of fears.
If the thorns have stuck me sometimes, I've good reason
  to suppose
It was to make me perk up, so's to 'preciate the rose.
So, I'm goin' to be thankful for the sunshine *and* the
  rain,
For the things that make me happy, for the purgin' done
  by pain;
For the love o' little children; for the friends that have
  been true;
For the guidin' hand that led me every threatnin'
  journey through.

Rabbi Alfred Wolf

Our Double Portion

Jewish and American history parallel each other in
many important respects. Both begin with painful
periods of subjection to powerful and exacting
peoples—the Israelites to Pharaoh and the Americans to
George III. True, the character and severity of the
bondage in the two cases differed. The children of Israel

124

were forced into back-breaking labor and were subjected to the humiliation of hard taskmasters; the American colonists were subjected to unfair treatment (such as taxation without representation) which they regarded as a humiliating form of bondage. Nevertheless, both peoples craved for freedom and independence.

Further, both the Jewish and the American people embarked upon their careers by making a covenant, dedicating themselves to the high ideals of liberty and humanity. The Covenant of the children of Israel is the Torah, the divine law, highlighted by the Ten Commandments which open with the proclamation: "I am the Lord, your God, Who brought you forth from the land of Egypt, from the house of bondage." The covenant of the American people, the Constitution of the United States of America and the inspired Declaration of Independence, highlight the ideals of "life, liberty and the pursuit of happiness."

Also, both the American and Jewish people had to deal with slavery problems. Here, too, the differences between the two are considerable. Yet, the points of similarity stand out most strikingly. The United States permitted, and even encouraged, the institution of slavery; the Constitution had not forbidden it. Thus, Negroes in large numbers were imported from Africa to the Southern states and used as slaves. Later on, the nation was torn apart and almost bled itself to death over this critical problem. President Lincoln gave utterance to the tragedy in his Second Inaugural Address. Recall his moving, almost prophetic words: "if God wills it that it [the war] continues until all the wealth piled by the bondmen's two hundred-and-fifty years of unrequited toil shall be sunk, and with every drop of blood drawn with the lash shall be paid by another drawn with the sword, as was said three thousand years ago, so still it must be said: 'The judgments of the Lord are true and righteous altogether.'"

The ancient State of Israel never imported slaves. Indeed, the Torah limited the practice of slavery to a minimum. It allowed a Hebrew to sell himself into servitude for a maximum of six years, either to pay a debt or to provide for his impoverished family. It can be readily seen that this type of servitude has little in common with slavery. The master's rights were restricted by the Torah, and even more so by Talmudic authorities. Hence, it was held that "slavery under such conditions was a greater burden to the master than to the slave."

Our prophet Jeremiah tells us that at one time even ancient Israel suffered from the curse and abuse inherent in slavery. The last king of Judah prevailed upon the powerful groups in Jerusalem to enter into a covenant, proclaiming the release of all Hebrew slaves, regardless of the time of servitude. Under pressure (the enemy stood practically at the gates of the city) the princes agreed to free the slaves. However, no sooner had the critical situation changed for the better, than the slaves were forced back into servitude, in complete disregard of the covenant.

Jeremiah, faithful to God and fearless of men, spoke out against the evil of slavery and chastised the greedy

126

and heartless masters. Lincoln might well have used these scorching words of the incensed prophet: "But you turned and you profaned My [God's] name . . . you brought them into subjection, to be slaves unto you. . . . And I will deliver the men who have violated My covenant . . . into the hand of the enemies. . . ." Indeed, the Great Emancipator sounded such a solemn note in his Second Inaugural Address.

Such then are the parallels of Jewish and American history. Both were conceived as nations dedicated to high ideals, and born in struggle for freedom and independence. Both have cherished the binding covenants (one divine, the other inspired) to guide their destinies. Both peoples have been again and again tested whether they have retained their loyalty to the faith of their fathers. History proves that with all the setbacks and frequent back-slidings, America has come through its trials and tribulations, often scarred, but always strengthened and prepared to carry on the glory of its adventure in freedom. The Jewish people has even more, surely for a longer period, withstood the tests to which it has been subjected again and again. Yet the Torah remains our eternal guide, freedom our great ideal, and human equality our steady goal.

How fortunate for us to be heirs to two great heritages which testify to the glory of God and the dignity of man.

Rabbi Solomon D. Goldfarb

* * *

127

Love and Faith

We live in a world of jets, nuclear physics, and space sattelites. But with all the new inventions around us, my favorite story is many thousands of years old. Long ago, there lived in the land of Canaan two brothers, owners of two small pieces of land. One of them was childless, but well-to-do; the other could hardly eke out a living for his large family of hungry children.

One night the rich brother could not fall asleep. He tried counting sheep, but he was too worried about his brother, and sleep would not come. "How can my poor brother," thought he, "feed the many mouths in his household from a parcel of land no bigger than mine?" He arose from his bed, went out into the field, gathered sheaves of wheat and began walking toward his brother's home.

That night, the poor brother also tossed and turned. He was overwhelmed with concern for the future of his childless brother. Again and again the question flashed through his tired mind: "Who will care for my brother in his old age? I am poor but I have children to comfort me in the twilight years of my life. Who will soothe the aches and pains of his old age?" What could he do to help? He got out of bed, went out into the field, filled his arms with all the sheaves of wheat he could find and began the trek to his brother's house.

Alone, in the darkness of the night the brothers met. There was no need for words of explanation. In the eloquent silence of that precious moment, the two

128

brothers embraced, tears rolling from their eyes.

But the two brothers were not alone. The Almighty One, looking on from above was moved by this beautiful act of brotherly love. "This piece of land upon which they met," He declared, "shall be sanctified forever." And indeed, centuries later, the Temple of Jerusalem was built on that very spot.

But this lovely story does not end with the Temple, for it has served to remind us ever since, that our own sanctuary of faith, rituals, and observances must stand on a foundation of selfless devotion and brotherly love.

Rabbi Hershel Cohen

* * *

The Rooster and the Bat

There is a wonderful story in the Talmud about a rooster and a bat. It was nighttime and the bat was boasting that he could see everything clearly, even though it was dark. The rooster felt very much inferior. He couldn't see a thing. How is it that God so blessed the bat that he could see clearly at night while he, the rooster, could only grope his way around, falling and bumping into things. As the night wore on, the rooster felt more and more unhappy about what he took to be a handicap. Finally, he fell asleep.

When the first rays of sun began to shine upon the beautiful countryside, the rooster awakened, stretched his legs, and broke forth into song. He looked for his friend, the bat, but he was nowhere to be found. It was then that the rooster realized how fortunate he was to be a rooster and not a bat. Said the happy rooster, "When the light comes, I begin to sing. But the bat has to hide from the light."

This story has an important meaning. There are people who are very happy when things are "dark." These are the people who lie and steal, and who take advantage of other people. They hit you and run away. They take things while you are not looking. They tell you one thing and mean another. These are the "night people." They are like the bat. But what happens to these people when truth comes? What happens to them when the light comes? They have to run away and hide.

Some of us are like the rooster. We are jealous of the people who seem to be successful when they lie and steal. We are jealous of the people who seem to be rich even though they get their money by doing things that are not nice. We wish sometimes that we could push other people around and do whatever we want to do. We are jealous of the people who are rough and tough. But, then, like the rooster, we get that wonderful feeling when we do something to help somebody. When we tell the truth, we become proud that we live best in the light, and not in the darkness, and like the rooster, we want to burst out in song.

Many stories we know are like the story of the bat and the rooster. In the Purim story Haman is the bat and

130

Mordecai is the rooster. Haman is happy when he thinks that his dark and evil plan will succeed, but it is Mordecai who is happy when the light of truth comes and the King learns about Haman's plans. Some of your parents remember the time of Senator McCarthy, who with his false charges frightened most Americans into believing what he said and accepting his teaching. But when the truth came out, Senator McCarthy was discredited and was censured by the U.S. Senate. He, too, was like the bat who has to hide when the light comes.

The problem, however, is that you can't always tell who is the bat and who is the rooster. You have to learn how to look and to listen closely. A person can be judged only on the basis of his deeds over a long period of time. Sometimes a bat, an evil person, will try to crow like a rooster, and you will have to judge his true personality for yourself; but judging other people is the most difficult of all things. It is very easy to make a mistake.

One thing we must try to do, however. Each of us must try to be sure that he is like the rooster. That is, each of us must try, to the best of his ability, to live in the light, and to be as truthful and helpful as he can be.

Rabbi Herbert M. Baumgard

* * *

The Ugly Duckling

Once upon a time a mother duck laid several eggs, out of which hatched beautiful ducklings. Every one gathered around the mother to congratulate her upon her good fortune. How lucky she was to have such lovely children! The mother duck would glide around the lake like a regal queen with her children swimming behind her like soldiers marching in a line. Then, when the little ducks became tired, the mother would stop to rest and bathe her little ones.

One day after such a trip across the lake, the mother noticed what seemed to be an extra child. This child was just as little as the rest; but unlike the others, she was not pretty at all. In fact, judged by normal duck standards, she was downright ugly. The mother was confused. Was this ugly duckling really part of her family? It seemed to her that originally there had been only four children; but, then again, maybe threre had been five, and she hadn't really noticed. Anyhow, this fifth child was certainly different, mostly because she was not at all pretty like the others. All the other fowls swimming in the lake also noticed the difference in the fifth child, and soon they were saying, "Look, here comes Mother Duck with her four beautiful ducklings and that Ugly Duckling."

You can well imagine how the fifth child must have felt. She saw everybody smiling when they looked at her brothers and sisters, but when they looked at her, they frowned. Tears ran down her face. What had she done that people didn't like her? It wasn't her fault that she wasn't pretty. After all, she was born that way.

Some of us are like this poor Ugly Duckling. We don't seem to be as pretty as other people. For example, some of us have a long nose, others have big ears; some of us are too tall, and others are too short. And then, some people are born reasonably pretty, but, as they grow older, something happens in their life that makes them less attractive. For example, some us lose the hair on our head, and we look at other people with thick wavy hair, and we say, "Gee, I wish I could be pretty like them." Or some of us may not be able to do things as well as other people can do them. For example, some of us can't run as fast as other people; or we can't dance as well as others, and we say, "Gee, I wish I could dance like they do." Or some of us can't sing as well as others, and some of us can't make as much money as other people. Almost all of us are Ugly Ducklings in one way or another. None of us is good and pretty in all things. No matter how pretty or capable we are, there is always something where somebody else is a great deal better than we are, and each of us says, "Gee, I wish I could be like that person." So we can understand how that poor Ugly Duckling felt as she swam around the lake with her brothers and sisters and knew that everybody was saying, "Look, how pretty those other ducks are."

Well, a strange thing happened on that lake that people still talk about to this very day. As the weeks and months went by, and the baby ducks grew larger and larger, people began to notice more and more that the Ugly Duckling was different. Finally, as the baby ducklings grew up, the Ugly Duckling seemed suddenly to change into the most beautiful of them all, and people

133

understood that the Ugly Duckling was not a duck at all. She was actually a Swan, and there is no fowl more beautiful than a grown Swan. With her neck curved gracefully and her brilliant white feathers gleaming in the sun, the grown Swan swam around the lake with her brothers and sisters, and she heard people saying, "Could that indeed be the Ugly Duckling? My, she has become more beautiful than all the rest. Look, how proudly she holds her neck. See how lovely her feathers are." The Ugly Duckling, now grown into a beautiful Swan swam around and did not let the people know that she could hear their compliments, for the Ugly Duckling had learned a very important lesson. She had learned that what seems at first to be ugly and not as good as other things, may, in time, become more beautiful and better than these things. So, if you are worried that you are not as pretty as someone else, or if you are worried that you may not be as good as someone else, just remember the story of the Ugly Duckling. Remember that if you keep working to improve yourself, the time will come when people will say to you, "My, she has become nicer than all the rest."

If you know boys and girls, who seem to be like the Ugly Duckling, if you see people laughing at them, try to help them. The time will come when the Ugly Duckling will grow up to be a beautiful Swan.

The truth is that we are all Ugly Ducklings in some ways, but we are also beautiful Swans in hiding.

Rabbi Herbert M. Baumgard

* * *

The Stiff-Necked People

In the Bible we can find many interesting and absorbing stories. Some are sad, some amusing, others are bewildering, leaving us wondering about their true meaning.

In one weekly portion we read a very puzzling narrative. It is so strange as to sound incredible. And yet it is true.

A few weeks after the children of Israel left Egypt, they received the Ten Commandments from God on Mount Sinai. Immediately after that great event, Moses went back to the mountain in order to receive more of the laws and precepts which belong to the Torah. In fact, it took Moses a long time to receive the whole of the Law. He spent forty days and forty nights on Mount Sinai before he was ready to come back to the camp where the Jewish people lived.

Now imagine the great surprise, indeed the shock Moses had when he came back. As he came closer, he noticed that the Jewish people were celebrating. He wondered what the reason for this festivity might be. As he drew nearer the true situation became clear to him. The children of Israel had made a golden calf! They had placed it in the middle of the camp, and were dancing around it and worshipping it! They even shouted that it had brought them out of Egypt! No wonder Moses felt so sad and angry that he broke the two tablets of stone which he was carrying in his hands.

When we finish reading the story we ask, how could it have happened? How was it possible that the children of

Israel should have forgotten all the miracles that God had performed for them? They had seen the plagues that were sent upon the Egyptians, had taken part in the miracle at the Red Sea, had heard the voice of the Almighty proclaim the Ten Commandments!

The Rabbis say that the people of Israel are stubborn. Already Moses had called them "stiff-necked." This means that it is not easy to bend or change them.

After living with the Egyptians for centuries, the Jewish people had in many ways become very much like them. They were partial to idols. All the miracles God had performed were still not sufficient to change their condition completely. That explains the golden calf. But once the Jews learned to accept God Almighty as the only true God, they remained faithful to Him throughout the ages. No matter how hard it was for them to keep the Jewish religion, they did it because they remained a stiff-necked people.

A verse in the Book of Proverbs (27:3) reads: "The stone is heavy and the sand is weighty; but the wrath of the wicked is heavier than both." The actual Hebrew words also allow for the following translation: "The stone is hard, the sand is soft and movable, but the wrath of the wicked is worse than both."

The latter translation offers an interesting explanation. A stone is very hard and cannot easily be broken. But once it is broken, it remains broken forever. On the other hand, in a heap of sand it is very easy to bring about a change. You need only touch it with your fingers and the whole heap of sand starts to shift and move. But once it becomes quiet again it will look exactly the same

as before. All the movement and upheaval is unnotice-
able a second later. The change can be brought about
quickly, but it is only a momentary change.

Different people have different natures and disposi-
tions. One person may be easy to persuade. You need
only talk to him for a little while and he will accept your
advice. He will very likely also soon change his mind
again. He is like the heap of sand. Any approach made
to him will influence him for the time being. A little
while later, however, he will again be exactly as he was
before.

But there is also the other type of person whom you
cannot easily convince. You will have to talk to him for
a long, long time before he is prepared to see your point
of view. Once he accepts it, however, he is likely to
remain convinced. He will keep to the new idea for a
very long time. He is like the stone which is hard to
break, but once broken will remain so for all time. The
wicked person, says Solomon in the Proverbs, has the
bad and weak points of both the stone and the sand. He
is as hard to convince as the stone is to be broken. He is
also as shifty as the sand and will return quickly to his
evil ways.

Having accepted the religious way of life, the Jews
are not likely to give it up. At times, it may look as if
many of the Jewish people forget and give up their
religious traditions. Yet there are always a few at least
who carry out all the precepts, the customs and laws as
our forefathers have done for many hundreds of
generations now.

These few people are the link in the long chain of

137

Judaism which connects the past with the future. It is a great privilege to belong to the fine traditional chain and to add a ring to it.

You, too, should try to take your place there. You know how you can do it. It is very simple. Keep to the traditional ways of Judaism. In them you will find a meaning for the past, contentment for the present, and glory for the future.

Rabbi Gerald Kaplan

* * *

God's Special Room

Where does God live? If God is the Lord over all, how does He choose a house? Many of you have often asked me that question. And it's a good one. Look around you, to the right and to the left. Yes God is here, and there, and there also. Yet, if God is everywhere, where shall we meet Him in prayer and worship?

Long ago our ancestors asked the same question and found a workable answer. Since God instructed Moses to build a tent of meeting, a portable ark, and to appoint servants to assist his brother Aaron with the priesthood, there must have been a House of God. The glory of God filled this Tabernacle. God was dwelling with his people.

138

Today we call the House of God a sanctuary. Sanctuary means a "holy place," a special area devoted to God. God is everywhere, true enough, but He is right here now with us at this moment in His House, in His Sanctuary. I like to call this section of our Temple, "God's Special Room." In the quiet beauty of our Ark, in the silence of this holy room God is here. Nothing but prayer, study, or assemblies like this one go on in this room devoted to God.

Somehow when we come into this room a feeling of quietness comes over us. We seem to shut out the noise of the outside. We are God's guests. "Reverence My Sanctuary" (Leviticus 26:2) is the commandment we are taught. If we talk, or act silly, or forget where we are, God might not stay. When you invite friends to visit, you expect them to be orderly. In the same way, God expects us to present our best selves. Reverence means respect. But often the feeling of reverence is lost on one disrespectful person.

And if we are respectful, then "honor and majesty are before Him; strength and beauty are in His sanctuary" (Psalms 96:6). We have made ourselves worthy children to the Father of fathers in His House. We find out just who we are, and what we must be, His helpers and partners in making this world a workshop for His name. Whenever we are in this room, we feel that sheltering love of God. Your conduct in the sanctuary has a voice. It's not heard, but it speaks even when you are silent. It tells of your belief in God, and what you think of your purpose. Your silent speech is your most precious prayer. If you wish to show your best behavior here then

139

it would be natural for you to want to show your best behavior outside in God's world.

If you pray for money, or honor, or something for yourself alone, you show God that you are selfish and alone. But if you want strength to help your neighbor, understanding to answer the problems of the world, and help to finish the tasks of reducing sickness and evil, God is here to listen. Your desires are your prayers. They are the pulses of our soul. Just as father and mother listen to what we want, so God hears our wishes and answers. How we act outside His room, how we live our desires will reflect God's influence upon us.

Yes, God dwells in this special room. He is everywhere, but at this very moment He is with me here. He can see through the respect I show Him, He can listen to my prayers, for what I wish for others, not only for myself. He will answer me outside the sanctuary in the way I will live His teaching.

Make your words like those of the Psalmist, "My heart standeth in awe of Thy words." (Psalm 119:161)

Rabbi Arnold G. Kaiman

* * *

The Power of the Tongue

Long ago, in a far-off land, lived a king who was wise and just, and deeply beloved by his subjects. To the great distress of his people, the king took sick and no one knew what ailed him. Day by day he grew weaker. In alarm, a call went out to the outstanding physicians in the realm to come to the palace for an urgent conference. For three days they examined, studied, and debated. Finally, they came to a unanimous decision. The only thing that could save the life of the king was milk taken from a lioness, and it was urgent that this be done as soon as possible. Notices were immediately posted in every prominent place, announcing that whoever would bring lioness' milk to the king would be given a title and the beautiful princess in marriage.

Many youths ventured forth to the jungles in search for a cure for their beloved monarch. Some of them never returned. The others all came back empty-handed. It is difficult to capture a live lioness, and a dead one cannot be milked. And even if she were captured, who could get close to this fierce wild beast to milk her without being clawed to death?

Among those who started out on this perilous journey was a youth who was sick with worry for his beloved king, and he resolved to achieve the success denied the others. He traveled a long distance into the jungle on horseback. Growing tired, he dismounted, seated himself under a tree, ate some of the food he had taken along, grew drowsy and fell fast asleep. Suddenly there broke forth a roar. The youth awoke from his deep slumber with a start. It was a strange, peculiar kind of roar. Mixed with it was great pain, as though the animal had been deeply hurt. Opening his eyes wide, the youth saw a lioness standing only a few feet away from him, holding up her paw, with tears streaming down her face. For the most sensitive part of the body of a lioness is the paw. There, right in the center of it was a big, sticky thorn. The beast stood there with pleading eyes, begging the youth to pull out the thorn and bring her relief. Pity for the animal drove away his fears, and with one swift sudden jerk, he pried the thorn loose. After that, the youth had no difficulty filling up a bottle with lioness milk, while the grateful beast licked his hand with gratitude.

Overjoyed by his success, the youth remounted his horse and flew toward the palace. But he had traveled so far that nightfall overtook him. He stopped at a wayside inn, and decided to spend the night there promising himself to be off with the crack of dawn.

That night, the youth's sleep was troubled by an extraordinary dream. He dreamed that all the limbs of his body were walking, talking, shouting, quarreling. Each one claimed credit for getting the cure for the king. "Had we not heard of the king's illness," said the ears, "none of us would have known about it." "Had we not carried the body, had we not milked the lioness," chimed in the legs and arms in turn, "we would not have moved nor would we have obtained the milk." Each of them tried to outshout the others, pressing his claims, insisting that he were most important to the enterprise. The last one to speak up was the tongue. When the others grew weary and the noise subsided, the tongue spoke simply, quietly and firmly, saying, "I am more important than all of you put together." Whereupon the other limbs burst out laughing. "What did you have to do with all this? Did you hear like the ears, see like the eyes, walk like the legs, milk like the arms? Where do you come off to boast and brag that you are the most important part of the body?" But the tongue answered softly, "You just wait and see."

The following morning, the youth awoke with a start as the sun was just coming up. He was disturbed and perplexed by this strange dream and what it could possibly mean. But then he remembered the bottle he had placed under his pillow for safekeeping, and all anxious thoughts flew out of his mind. Quickly, he gathered up his belongings, jumped on his horse and was off to the palace with the wind.

The palace guards stopped him when he arrived and demanded to know what business had taken him to court. Holding up the bottle, he exclaimed exultingly, "I hold in my hand the cure for the king." He was swiftly rushed to the bedside of the king who, by this time, was so weak that the pallor of death was on his face. "Draw near, my son," whispered the king, in a voice so faint that he could hardly be heard, "and tell me what you have in your hand." Bending forward the youth replied, "I hold dog's milk." A dark look of fury came over the face of the king. Who was this miserable upstart who dared to come right up to his dying monarch to mock his illness to his face? "Away with him," motioned the king. Orders were given that the youth be cast into a dungeon and hanged in the public square in the morning as a lesson and a stern warning to those who dare trifle with the king's illness.

That night, the unhappy youth had another terrible

dream. Once more, the limbs of his body went about talking, shouting, screaming, but there was terror in their voices. For they knew this was to be their last night on earth. "It's all your fault," they said as they turned upon the tongue. "You deliberately twisted the words in the mouth to make those words come out that have brought us to the point of death. You've got to do something about this." The tongue smiled and said, "See, didn't I tell you that I was the most important part of the body? With me lies the power of life and death." "Yes, yes, you are right," shouted the ears and eyes, and legs and arms, "you are absolutely right. But get us out of this; get us out of this." "Don't worry," promised the tongue, "I got you into this, I'll get you out."

The next morning a huge crowd gathered to watch the hanging in the public square. It's sad to note that there are many people who get pleasure in watching others suffer. So the square was packed. Even the king had himself propped up in his bed and moved close to the window to witness the execution.

The young man, with his hands tied behind his back, mounted the steps of the scaffold, and was brought forward to stand under the gallows. Now, there was a hallowed tradition in that kingdom that a person about to be executed was given a chance to make one last statement if he wished. As they were about to blindfold the luckless youth before lowering the rope around his neck and shoulders, the captain of the guard asked him if he wished to say anything. "Yes," replied the youth. Stepping forward the better to be heard and addressing

144

the king whom he could see through the open window, he said, "Your Majesty, I beg your humble pardon for what I said to you yesterday. I don't know whatever possessed me that the words got twisted in my mouth. I must have been worn out from the long journey. What I really held in my hand was a bottle containing, not dog's milk, but milk taken from a lioness." A hush settled on the crowd. Soon this was succeeded by murmurs that grew louder and louder. "This is a trick, " they said. "He is lying just to save his miserable neck. Hang him." But the doctors attending the king took a different view. Perhaps the youth was telling the truth. The king was so close to death, only a miracle could save him now. Maybe the cure was in the bottle. What could the youth gain by such a foolish deception? Another twenty-four hours? So they persuaded the king to postpone the execution for a day while the remedy was being tested. At the end of a day, the execution was put off for a month, and at the end of the month, the king was on his feet again dispensing justice and hailed by his loving subjects. The youth was made into a prince, married the princess and lived happily ever after. Thus did all men learn the truth in the statement of the author of the Book of Proverbs that "Death and life are in the power of the tongue" (Proverbs 18, 21).

Rabbi Phillip L. Lipis

* * *

Our Wonderful Treasures

Three men were riding on camels in the desert when suddenly they heard a voice call out: "Halt! Get off your camels!" Frightened, they looked around but they could see no one. They continued on their journey when again the voice called out, "Halt! Get off your camels!" This time, shaking from head to foot, they alighted from their camels as the voice had commanded. Then the voice said, "Prostrate yourselves upon the sand," and they immediately obeyed. "Now take as much sand in your hands as you possibly can," which they did. "Now stand up, climb back on your camels and continue riding, but do not open your hands until dawn breaks. At that time, when you open your hands, you will be both happy and sad." The three men stood up, jumped back on the camels, clenched their fists ever tighter, afraid to open them, and rode as fast as they could in order to get away from the mysterious voice. When dawn broke, they opened their hands and instead of sand they found precious jewels and gems. This sight made them happy, but at the same time it made them sad. They were happy that they obeyed the voice and had taken the sand because they were now rich. But they were sad because they did not take more sand and thus become even richer.

Many of us are like the men in our story. All of us who study in a religious school are in a very fortunate position. We are being given a Jewish education that will prepare us to take our rightful place in the life of the temple and Jewish community when we grow older. We will be educated Jews and we will know the meaning, the significance, and the importance of our religion. We will know the background of our customs, ceremonies, history, and literature. But, as adults, when we look back to the education we received we will be both happy and sad. We will be happy that we had a Jewish education and that we know some of the beautiful things about our religion, but we will be sad because we did not take better advantage of the Jewish education that was given to us. Let us, therefore, study and work hard now, so that when we grow up and look back upon our Jewish education we will be happy to know we took full advantage of our opportunities.

Rabbi Bernard Zlotowitz

* * *

Who Is Your Brother—or Sister?

When I was your age, my folks lived in a mixed neighborhood in St. Louis, Missouri. It was an immigrants' section of the city. The older people had come from the Old World. Occasionally Christian and Jewish families did not get along well. But something happened to patch up things.

A year or so after we had moved into the neighbor-

147

hood, a few Negroes began settling there. Most of our neighbors did not like the idea of living close to colored people. One of these Negroes was a woman who had a small basement apartment on the corner, diagonally across the street from us. The whites talked and gossiped about that "colored woman." After listening to much talk, I, too, began to resent her.

About that time my father bought me a bicycle as a gift. I must admit that I had a hard time learning how to ride the pesky thing. I fell off many times and injured myself where it really hurts.

One summer afternoon, when I thought I had finally gotten the knack of it, and was proudly riding down the block, the bicycle hit a rock and suddenly turned over and fell on top of me.

This happened at the very corner where the colored lady lived. I was badly hurt, or so I felt, and cried out. Some of the kids and even adults who saw the accident laughed. I suppose they thought the whole thing was a joke. I looked so funny squatting in the middle of the street and trying clumsily to get out from under the bicycle.

Just then, through my tears, I saw dark hands lift the bicycle off me. The same dark hands also helped me up. Guiding the bicycle with one hand, the colored lady led me with the other onto her humble stoop. She seated me, washed my wounds, applied medicines, and put bandages on my sores. She gave me a glass of nice, cold milk, and said: "You'll be all right, boy. Don't fret. Now I guess I better take you home. Your mom might be worried about you." And so she did.

148

She turned me and my bicycle over to my mother who was looking for me on the front steps. My mother thanked her. She had guessed what had happened. She asked the Negro lady whether she could do anything for her. The woman smiled pleasantly and said: "It's all right ma'am. I don't want nothing. Glad I could help your boy." She paused for a moment, turned to me and said: "Be careful, boy. Don't let it happen again. I might not be around." I thanked her lamely as she turned to leave.

During that period, I had been studying the Bible in Hebrew at my cheder (Hebrew School). Only a couple of days before I had read the words of the prophet Malachi,

> Have we not all one Father?
> Hath not one God created us?
> Why do we deal treacherously
> every man against his brother?

When I first learned the Hebrew words, I was not at all sure that I knew what they really meant. Now the meaning became clear to me. I am sure you children also know what they stand for.

At home, recovering from my accident, I asked myself: "Who is my brother? Who is my sister?" I knew the answer.

Rabbi Samuel Teitelbaum

* * *

What, Again?

Tonight I want to tell you a story of a boy who lived many years ago. Now this little boy had a nickname. People get nicknames in different ways. This boy had a favorite expression he used so often that people called him by it. When his mother asked him to do the dishes he would say: "What, again?" And when his father asked him to cut the lawn he would say: "What, again?" And when it came time to go to school he would say: "What, again?" So soon everybody called him What Again. Now What Again really enjoyed doing things once. But not more. When a fair came to his town he went once, but nothing could persuade him to go a second time.

What Again had a little black dog. They were great friends, in fact, they were a lot like each other. This little black dog was a watchdog, but he would bark only once. It was a long, loud bark, but only one. When people said to Only Once, (for that was the dog's name), "Why don't you bark more?" he would say, "But I've already barked." So you see What Again and Only Once were perfect for each other.

Things went on and What Again and Only Once continued to be difficult. Often What Again's father asked him to cut the grass but he would only cut it at the beginning of the year. Then the grass grew higher and higher until it was taller than a person. The weeds grew five, six, seven feet tall. The backyard was like a jungle.

150

It was so overgrown that only What Again and Only Once cared to walk there.

One day What Again and Only Once were walking in the tall grass and weeds when they heard a great roar. It was a big lion. Only Once gave his one bark, but it was a scared one. What Again trembled. "Who are you?" he asked. "I am a lion, and you are my lunch,"said the lion. That didn't make What Again feel too happy. "But lions don't belong in backyards," he said. "This is a jungle," said the lion. "I'm from India, and I got lost, and this is the first jungle I've found. I'm at home here!" Then big tears fell down the faces of What Again and Only Once. The lion said "Why are you crying? Lions have to eat too." "I'm crying," said the boy, "because now that I've learned my lesson it's too late. I should have cut the grass again and again. From now on I want to do everything more than once."

At that there was a twinkle in the eye of the lion, for he was really a tender creature. He took out a big ruler, looked at What Again and at the ruler, and said to What Again: "Take off your shoes." And What Again did. Then the lion measured him and said: "Half an inch too small. According to our rules, we lions can't eat anyone unless they are big enough. You are lucky."

Only Once barked a happy bark. And What Again jumped up and down. And he said "From now on I'm going to do the dishes again and again. And I'll cut the lawn every week. And I'll go again and again to religious school."

The lion then said: "You have learned a lesson. Whatever is good in life, you have to do lots of times.

Just like the sun has to shine every day so the food will grow; just as the rain has to fall again and again so the grass will be green; just as the stars have to shine every night so we won't be lonely. In the same way we have to do all important things again and again."

So What Again no longer said, "What, again?" And he did his duties and went to religious school with no more complaints.

Tonight we follow the advice of the lion. For it is our holiday of Simchas Torah, which means, being happy because of the Torah. Tonight we finish the last book of the Torah, and do you know what we do? We start right again at the beginning. For as What Again learned, whatever is important we must do often. And because the Torah is so important and good we start at the beginning as soon as we reach the end.

Rabbi Norman D. Hirsh

* * *

Not a Minute to Lose

A famous French general who had worked very hard all his life finally reached the age of retirement. It was then that the government paid him just to enjoy life and to do the things he wanted to do.

It was his very first day of retirement. He was in the

152

courtyard behind his house, getting ready to plant a tree. He was just about to lift his shovel, when the doorbell rang and his secretary came to him to tell him that Mrs. Fontaine had come to have tea with him.

"Who invited her?" asked the general. He was annoyed.

"I once told her to drop in if she were ever in the neighborhood and here she is in the parlor, waiting to have tea with you."

"Well, tell her she will have to come back tomorrow. I have been waiting for years to plant this tree and I am not going to wait any longer."

"But, General, she is a very important person and you really should see her."

"Can't I see her tomorrow? What's the big hurry?"

"Why not today? What is so important?"

"I'm planting a tree and that's important to me. I've waited for years for a free moment to do this, and I intend to do it now."

"But General, even if you planted that particular tree now, it would take fifty years before it bore fruit. What difference does one more day make?"

"That settles it," said the general, "if it will take fifty years before this tree will bear fruit, then I must plant it right this minute. I will not see anyone until I have planted this tree. I haven't got a minute to lose."

A philosopher once said that the secret of life lies in learning to plant a tree whose fruit you will never eat, whose shade you will never see. When you learn to plant things you yourself will never use, you will understand how this world works.

The things that you want done, you yourself must do. But the things which you do should not only be those which bring immediate results. Sometimes the greatest magic takes centuries. The trees which Jews plant on Tu BiShevat have that kind of magic.

If every Moslem planted one tree a year in the Sahara desert, it would be the world's most beautiful orchard. There are 400 million Moslems in the world. There are only 14 million Jews. A good Jew should plant one tree a year, one tree whose fruit he will never eat, whose shade will bless only others. We haven't a moment to lose.

Rabbi Leonard Winograd

* * *

To Be a Jew

One of the most dramatic statements in the Bible is the brief declaration made by the prophet Jonah, who when asked by an angry and frightened ship's crew, "Who are you?" replied simply: "I am a Jew."

The world has not ceased, nor will it cease asking of each of us, "What does it mean to be a Jew?" The question may spring forth from the lips of our non-Jewish friends, it may be put to us in a spirit of hatred and animosity by an anti-Semite, or it may even be posed by our own inquisitive and curious children. No matter who asks it, it is a question that will be asked and we are held accountable to answer.

We have heard much and we will continue to hear more about the so-called "vanishing" American Jew. Personally, I will begin to worry about the Jew vanishing, only when the Jew, by word and by action, becomes unwilling or unable to give a meaningful and intelligent answer to the question "What is a Jew?"

Too often, we who are Jews tend to take our Jewish origins so much for granted that we completely over-look not only the past magnificence of our cultural, spiritual, and ethical heritage, but also the present and future responsibilities and obligations that being a Jew places upon us. It is as if after being told for so long by our admirers that we are the chosen people, or the people of the book, or the original pioneers in monotheism, that we have come to accept all these praises as our just due, without any thought for the ongoing effort and the concentrated will that is needed to justify these honors. Ask and define for yourselves; what does it mean to me to be a Jew?

Recently I came across the following words written by Rabbi James Heller, as he sought to define what it meant for him to be a Jew:

> To be a Jew. . .
> It is to look back over one's shoulder at patriarch, prophet and psalmist.
> It is to feel about the earth the presence of one's brothers bound to one in deep ways. Even if I wish to

repudiate them, the world will not let me. Tragedy binds me to them even when dreams do not.

It is to be the result of a severe process of selection, to be the scion of those who have breasted the billows of ages.

It is to feel many things blended in one's heart; people, faith, mission, martydoms. Fear is in it for the weak, glory for the strong, confusion for the bewildered and clear vision and simple faith for the stout of heart.

It is to love one's own people and to know that this love conflicts in no way with utter loyalty to lands like America which have given us liberty and equality.

It is to realize that one has been chosen to be a touchstone of the progress of the human soul, to live through some days that witness the recrudescence of the evil in men, to see it wreak itself upon my people.

Israel is partly a legacy, partly a social entity, most deeply and fully a religion coextensive with life. It is all these fused into unity, into one way, one vision.

Israel is as diverse as life and as unitary as life; as plural as history and as consistent as God's purpose in history; as mysterious as the union and interaction of body and spirit.

This is my people and my faith which I love, and in which I take deep pride.

It is time that we stop taking both our Jewishness and our Judaism as a matter of simple ease and convenience. Judaism is more than just a simple accident of birth, a word to be used in filling in a religious preference questionnaire. It is not a set of beliefs to be stared at in amazement, as if they were objects in a curio shop or a group of household idols, before whose altar we pay

156

polite, albeit perfunctory obeisance.

It is time that we stopped playing the role of passive Jews willing to let the rabbi pray for us and satisfied to have the next person live Jewishly for us.

To be uncommitted is to be a Jew by proxy, and since when did we ever in our history insure the survival, let alone the strengthening of Judaism, by following the path of maximum indifference and minimum devotion?

If, on the other hand, we strive to become maximal Jews, then we will be able, with joy and with genuine conviction, to echo the words of Jonah, "I am a Jew." Jonah saw what we must recognize—that in order to be a believing and practicing Jew, Judaism demands of us not only undying group allegiance, but unswerving individual commitment as well. Then, not only for James Heller, but for each of us, Judaism *will* become the guiding force behind all our thoughts and acts, the people and the faith which we love, and in which we will have come to take deep and abiding pride.

Rabbi Samuel Weingart

* * *

Joseph, a Modern Youth

In one part of Genesis, the great personality of Joseph, the eleventh son of Jacob, comes to the forefront. He comes upon the Biblical scene as a youth, a teenager. As the Bible says: "These are the generations of Jacob, Joseph being seventeen years old."

Like most youngsters, Joseph was a dreamer. In fact, the course of his life seems to have been affected by dreams. Both the terrible tragedy which caused him to be separated from his family and, later, his rise to power and fame in Egypt were brought about by his tendency to dream.

In commenting on the statement "And he was a lad," Rashi asks, "Why does it have to tell us he was a lad? We understand from the statement that he was seventeen." What the Torah wants to emphasize is that Joseph would do the things a boy does, such as groom himself to appear handsome. In other words, he was a normal youngster. He probably loved sports and recreation.

However, the Torah also testifies to another side of Joseph's personality, as it is written: "Now, Israel loved Joseph more than all of his children, because he was a son of his old age." Another interpreter says, "He was a wise son to his father," meaning that whatever Jacob learned at academies he transmitted to his son Joseph. He loved Joseph because in him he saw hope for the future of Judaism. He loved him because he was able to instill in him a love of God's ways.

Although he left his father's house at a tender age and endured many trials, Joseph never forgot this training. Even later, when he became Viceroy of Egypt, the highest position in the land next to Pharaoh, he never forgot his obligations as a Jew. When he disclosed himself, he said, "I am Joseph, the same one you knew in the land of Canaan. I still observe Shabbat and the other Mitzvot."

Joseph's adherence to Judaism is also evident in his dreams. The first was about sheaves in the field. The second was about the sun, the moon, and the eleven stars. The first is symbolic of physical life, of daily activities which a person performs. The second dramatized the spiritual life which one must lead. In Joseph's own life there was no contradiction between heaven and earth. And this "mix" ought to be in everyone's life. One element must add to the other.

Jewish youngsters ought to imitate Joseph. Joseph was a normal youngster with all the familiar impulses of a lad his age. Yet, at the same time he was able to study and develop himself in his youth for the important obligations he was to shoulder later on.

You too, must take advantage of these vital years to develop yourselves as useful citizens and Jews. Like Joseph, it is not necessary to give up the attractions and enjoyments of youth, but rather to bring about a harmonious combination of both the physical and the spiritual. You may seek enjoyment, but also learn to find it in worship of God and service to His mandates.

Rabbi Maynard C. Hyman

* * *

159

Three Friends

It was a warm spring day when Danny and Fred were dismissed from their fifth-grade class in public school. Since kindergarten, they had been together in the same class every school day and, being neighbors, they walked together to and from school. On weekends they went their separate ways, Danny to his temple and Fred to his church. Many times they had talked about their religion and Fred talked frequently about heaven and hell. Danny had little to say on this subject for it was not discussed very much in temple.

On this day the two friends played tag as they headed for home. As usual, Flip, Danny's cocker spaniel, raced to meet his master. So happy was he that he failed to see the oncoming car as he dashed across the street. There was a screech of brakes, but it was too late. The right front wheel hit Flip's back. Danny ran to his wounded pet but there was little he could do. The dog died in Danny's arms.

In vain did Fred try to console his friend. As a last resort he assured him that Flip was a good dog and he was sure to go to heaven. When the first hours of grief had passed, Danny remembered the words of his friend. Would his dog truly go to heaven? It would be such a comfort to know. Did Jews believe in heaven? When Danny's father came to his room to console him he asked: "Dad, do we Jews believe in heaven?"

Danny's father was accustomed to his son's questions. He always managed to come up with an answer, even if he had to find it in the books or turn to the rabbi.

"Danny," began his father, "let me answer your question with a parable from the Talmud." Danny was familiar with this source of wisdom. The rabbi, his Hebrew- and Sunday-school teachers, and his father had often quoted from it. Anxious to be assured about the destiny of his canine friend, Danny was prepared to listen.

"A man named Benjamin had three friends," continued his father, "all of whom he treasured very much. He visited with them and enjoyed their company. On occasions of gladness they rejoiced together and in sadness they shared each other's sorrow. One day Benjamin was summoned to court. A terrible thing over which he had no control had befallen him. He called on his first friend and told him of his trouble. He appealed to him to accompany him to court for moral support. His friend was busy on a new venture and said he could not spare the time. Disappointed, Benjamin turned to his second friend. Imagine his chagrin when this friend, too, condescended to escort him up to the courthouse, but no further. Benjamin found it hard to understand his friends. In desperation he turned to his third friend. How close they had been to one another! He had never failed him in the past. It is not difficult to imagine Benjamin's joy when his third friend consented not only to go with him into court but to plead his case before the judge and try to obtain his acquittal."

There was a pause. Danny looked at his father quizzically. "That's a fine story, but what has it to do with heaven?"

His father continued: "Benjamin is everyman. At the time of his death every man has three friends. The first is his money and worldly possessions. In the face of death man calls upon everything he owns to save him. He would give everything for some assurance of peace as he prepares to meet his God. But his first friend, his wealth, turns him down cold.

"Filled with anxiety, he turns to his second friend. They are the members of his family and his intimate friends. They promise to escort him to the courthouse but no further. When a man dies his family and friends accompany him to the grave. They can go no further. They leave him alone and go their way.

"In desperation he turns to his third friend. They are his deeds of loving kindness, those beloved angels he created everytime he performed an act of charity, spoke a kind word, entered his place of worship, or did something worthwhile. The good deeds walk with man right up to the Heavenly Judge and plead his cause for him. One by one this friend spread out before the court all of man's good deeds, every service the man rendered, every kind word he spoke, until the judgment is passed: 'Your life has been one continuous benediction. You were a joy and blessing to all who knew you. Your reward in your lifetime was great, for what greater reward is there than the inner peace and satisfaction from the knowledge that your deeds found favor in the eyes of God and man. Go forth in peace, for your fellowmen will remember you in joy and peace and your future is assured.'"

Danny heaved a sigh of satisfaction. "You mean that

each man creates his heaven by his own good deeds, and. . ."

"That's exactly what I mean," said his father.

"Then, Flip too, has found his heaven, for I shall always remember him for the friendship and joy he brought me in his life."

"Precisely," answered his father, "and, now, sleep well, my son."

Danny closed his eyes with a smile on his lips, assured that his faithful friend had found his heaven.

Rabbi Abraham Ruderman

* * *

Ideals of a People

Many things can be learned about a people by reading its literature. Some nations live near water and their literature contains stories about fishermen or tales of the sea. Others live near deserts and their stories are of camels and oases. The Jew is noted for his faith in God despite persecutions through the ages. Jewish literature reflects these ideals.

Take for example, a stirring story by Isaac Leib Peretz. According to the story, a Jew once died and his soul flew up for judgment. The soul was ushered into a large room which contained a special kind of scale. On one side, they placed all the man's good deeds; on the other, they placed his bad ones. And, lo and behold, something happened which had never happened before; the good deeds of this man weighed exactly the same as the bad deeds. Since he could not enter Heaven unless the good deeds outnumbered the bad, the sad soul was just about to leave the judgment room, when the keeper suggested that he return to earth to look for three gifts that might be acceptable to the Heavenly Tribunal, and through these gifts secure his admission to Heaven. But what would be good enough to present to the Heavenly Tribunal?

The soul flew around earth for a long time and could find nothing. Then one day it saw a castle, and, inside, he saw that the owner was being robbed. The robbers in the treasure room were gathering up gold and silver and jewelry. One of the robbers held the owner of the castle with a knife at his throat. Surely the robbers would kill him if he but moved. Then suddenly, as the robbers took one of the chests, the owner of the castle lurched forward and was stabbed. Here was something very precious, more valuable than gold or silver, thought the soul, for the man gave up his life to protect it. And the soul flew down to look at the chest. Inside, there were no gems, no gold nor silver, but just a box of earth; earth from the land of Israel that was more precious than the gold and silver, for the man had wanted this earth to be placed below his head when he was buried. The soul took a grain of this earth to Heaven, and it was accepted as the first gift.

The second gift was even more difficult to find. After

many months of searching, the soul found a market place in which a huge crowd was assembled. In fact, it looked like a court was in session. As the soul flew nearer, it was able to discern that a young Jewess was on trial for appearing on the streets of the town during the Easter period. This was not permitted. As punishment for her ''crime'' she was to be tied to the tail of a horse and be dragged through the streets. She was granted one last wish, and requested a pin to tie her skirt. And so it was. The soul noted the modest wish of this girl and thought that the pin would make a fine gift. The soul took the pin and brought it to Heaven, and the second gift was accepted.

Now there was only one more gift to go. The soul saw a group of soldiers being issued whips and lining up in two rows facing each other. An old man was to pass between the rows and be whipped as punishment for a ''sin'' he had committed. The sin was that he remained a Jew. And while the soul was watching, the old Jew began to walk between these two lines of soldiers. All of a sudden one of the whips touched the man's yarmulke and it fell to the ground. Without hesitation, the man walked back to the yarmulke, despite the fact that he was subjected to many more lashes. This would be a fitting third gift, thought the soul, because this man was willing to accept the additional lashes of the whip to re-trieve a holy object. The third gift was accepted and the soul earned his right to enter Heaven.

Now this is a beautiful story and a simple one too. But within this story one can find the three foundations of Judaism, ideals which have held the Jews together.

165

One of these pillars of Judaism is our religious faith represented by the man who retrieved the yarmulke. For this man life was not worth living without his faith and belief. The young girl whose last request was the pin was putting the morals of Judaism into practice. A distinguishing mark of the Jew has been his righteousness, not only in regards to synagogue, but in his everyday life as well. The third pillar of Judaism is our love for the Land of Israel, represented in the story by the man who wanted to save the box of soil from Eretz Yisrael so that it could be placed under his head when he was buried. The love of Israel as the spiritual center of Judaism certainly has been a unifying force in Jewish tradition. For all of these ideals Jews were willing to give up their lives if necessary. Think for a moment, how important are these Jewish ideals in your life?

Rabbi Donald Frieman

* * *

Questions which Make One Wise

Do your parents sometimes become exasperated with you and say, "Stop asking so many questions?" I'm sure there are times when that happens to all of us, especially when our questions are meant to draw

166

attention to ourselves, not to obtain important information from our elders.

Once there was a king who wanted to become wise so he could help his people, and he thought of three questions whose answers would accomplish this purpose. We, too, should ask these questions, if we are to become smart and good. The questions were: "What is the most important time for every action? Who are the most important people with whom I am to concern myself? What is the most important thing I can do for them?"

The king offered a great reward for the answers, but no one, not even his wisest counselors could satisfy him with their many answers.

Now it happened that not far from the city there lived a hermit who was very wise, but usually only the common people came to him, never anyone as great as a king. The king heard about him and decided to dress in ordinary clothes and seek his answers. He drew near the hermit's hut, got off his horse, left it with his bodyguards, and went on alone.

The hermit, a feeble old man, was digging in his garden. The king went up to him and asked him if he could tell him the right time, person, and action, so that he might have no regret for having missed them. The old hermit listened but continued working, tired as he was, without saying a word. The king, who felt sorry for the old man, took the spade and started digging for him. After he too became tired, he returned the spade and said, "You have not answered my questions."

"There comes someone running!" exclaimed the

167

hermit. The king turned and saw a wild-eyed man, running with his hand on his side. As he reached them, he fell in a faint. Seeing that the man was wounded, they bandaged him and stopped the bleeding. When night came, the king, still awaiting an answer, fell asleep next to the injured man.

Early in the morning the wounded man awoke, and seeing the king, cried out: "Give me your pardon!" "I have nothing to pardon you for, I do not even know you," replied the king. "Know then, that I was your enemy; when I heard you were here alone, I planned to kill you, but as you stayed with the hermit so long I became impatient and left my hiding place. Your soldiers saw me and wounded me, but now you, whom I swore to kill, have saved my life. Pardon me and I will serve you the rest of my days." The king was happy to have made a friend of an enemy, pardoned him and sent him to his own doctor to be cared for.

And now as he was about to leave, the king asked the hermit, "For the last time, will you please answer my questions?" "They are already answered," said the hermit. "If yesterday you had not pitied my weakness and helped me dig, you would have left and been killed by that man. Therefore, the right time was when you took my spade, and I was the most important person, and the most important work was to help me out. When the stranger ran up the most important time was when you bandaged him for if you hadn't, he would have died without becoming your friend. Therefore he was the most important person, and what you did was the most important action." Thus we must remember: The most important time is *now*, for only the present time belongs to us; and the most important action is to do good to that person or for that person.

Rabbi Leo J. Stillpass

*   *   *

The Road to Thamara

Several years ago I had the privilege of joining an Israeli youth movement's Chanukah *tiyul* (expedition) to the Israeli Negev. For four days we hiked due south from Beersheba. We hiked from 5:00 in the morning until 7:30 at night, stopping only for meals. Not only did we hike at a very rapid pace, but the youngsters sang as they marched. I burned (blisters on my blisters) while they sang and danced.

Finally, on the fifth day, our leader (nineteen-year-old Elisha) announced to the group that the reason we had been hiking so many hours a day was to gain an extra day on our schedule so that we could explore an old road which he had noticed the year before while taking this trip. The road was quite a primitive one. We started along the sun-baked earth trail; the farther we went, the more indistinct it became. We traveled through mountain passes and around dried up *wadi*

169

(gully) beds until at about high noon, when the sun was directly overhead, we came to a fork in the road. As a matter of fact, the road divided into four new roads. We began to look for signs that would tell us the destinations of each road. Finally, one youth uncovered an old signpost which had been uprooted years before. Five signs were attached to the post, all written in Turkish-Arabic. Luckily, many of the youngsters had studied Arabic in school and could read the signs which read: Rimon, El Auja, Aquaba, Thamara, and Petra.

As you know, Israel becomes narrower and narrower as one goes south, and three out of five of the destinations were indeed perilous. El Auja is in the Sinai Peninsula, which was then part of Egypt. Petra is in the Hashemite Kingdom of Jordan, as is Aqaba the road to which might cross into Jordanian territory long before we reached the hostile destination. Rimon was where we had camped the night before, and Thamara was up in the central Negev, not far from S'de Boker, the kibbutz where Ben-Gurion had lived. Thus, only the road to Thamara would be a safe one for us. The question, of course, was which road led to Thamara. We thought and thought and finally one young man had a wonderful idea. He said, "All we have to do is orient the signpost. We know the road upon which we have traveled and we know that our starting point was Rimon. Thus all we have to do is put the signpost in the ground, orienting the Rimon sign to the road on which we traveled, and then we can find the road to Thamara."

Thus I say to you, my friends, that the only way we can find the road to Thamara (tomorrow) is to know the

170

road from whence we have come. Only a study of the Jewish past will lead us to an understanding of the present and the future.

Rabbi Henry F. Skirball

*   *   *

Every Little Bit Counts

Many years ago in Palestine there lived a man who was well-blessed by God. His silos were full of grain, his storage barns were filled with corn, his fields were green, and his flocks manifold and healthy. There was only one thing the man lacked and yearned for—a son and heir. He prayed to God and made a vow that if God would hearken to his prayer for a son he would gladly share of all his physical possessions with the poor and needy of the land.

In due time, we are told, his wife presented him with a baby son and he did not forget his promise to God. He sent his servants throughout the land, of Palestine inviting all to come to Jerusalem eight days hence for the naming of his son. He asked the people to bring empty yokes, empty sacks, and empty wagons so they could fill them with the bounty which God had given to him. He only made one request of the people in return,

171

that each one would bring a wineskin filled with the wine of his particular part of Palestine. The purple wines of the Sharon, the red wines of the Galilee, the white wines of the hills of Judea.

On the appointed day the roads up the hills of Judea were filled with people coming for the happy event. Each one had with him empty sacks, empty yokes, and empty wagons, and each one, as requested, had with him a wineskin. When they arrived in Jerusalem they saw erected a large water tower with a hole at the top into which one could pour wine and a faucet at the bottom from which one could draw off the wine. Each one climbed the ladder emptying the contents of his wineskin into the tower and then sat down waiting for the ceremony to begin. When all were seated, the host went to the faucet with a pitcher expecting a bouquet of wine for the Kiddush. Imagine his shock when he turned on the faucet and only water poured forth!

What had happened? Well, each person had looked at the large tower and said to himself, "What a gigantic tower! My tiny little bit of wine won't even be tasted amongst all the wine in the tower. I think I will go behind a house and drink the wine I brought and fill the wineskin with water. After all, what difference could it make amongst all that wine in that large tower." The trouble, of course, was that each person thought the same thing and the ceremony was spoiled.

Thus it is with the many things that must be done in life. We look at the large job to be done and say that our contribution would be insignificant and, therefore, we make no contribution at all. Judaism tells us not to water down our contribution but to act as if our small act would be the decisive one for the cause which we would serve.

Rabbi Henry F. Skirball

*   *   *

The War of the Plants

In the beginning God created the heaven and the earth, and there was peace upon earth. It was not until He created the fruits of the soil that discord entered our planet. Yes, from the very first the plant kingdom was divided into two warring camps. On one side were the Roly Polies and the other, the Skinny Malinks.

Who were the Roly Polies? Why they were the round oranges, the apples, tomatoes, potatoes, etrogs, and the like. The Skinny Malinks drew their fighting forces from the slender grasses, tall celery, stringbeans, asparagus, willow, and such. Only the trees remained neutral. It is not that they were so peace loving, but rather that they were unacceptable to either side. The Skinny Malinks, seeing their round bushy branches, suspected them of being Roly Polies, while the Roly Polies, concentrating on their long slender trunks, considered them Skinny Malinks. And so, they became the neutral mediators in the combat to follow.

173

Quickly the fighting forces armed. Armies of thistles and thorns were recruited from both sides. Roly Poly potatoes prepared to roll down hill with increasing power. Skinny Malink asparagus sharpened their spears.

The war was about to begin and might have destroyed all plant life if the neutral mediator, the tree, had not spoken up.

"Foolish plants," he chided them, "do you want to do as the humans do and wage a bloody war in order to have peace? If you must battle, let words be your weapons for they are the strongest weapons ever forged. Yet they cause no blood to shed. And if words are your weapons, you can enter the Kingdom the Most High and He Himself can mediate between you."

And so it was that the Skinny Malinks and the Roly Polies prepared to assemble before their Maker. Many preparations had to be made, many legal briefs typed, and most important of all, a spokesman on each side had to be chosen. For the Roly Polies this presented no problem. The fragrant etrog, symbol of all plants that both knew the law and practiced good deeds, was loved by all and was quickly nominated and elected. But the Skinny Malinks found themselves in danger of going to the nominating convention with their ranks divided between the palm, the myrtle, and the willow. The palm insisted that in a legal matter such as this, she, the symbol of plants who were learned in the law should certainly be chosen. Many, however, favored the myrtle. True, the myrtle knew little of the law but her good deeds were known far and wide, and it was thought only fitting to honor such saintliness by proclaiming her leader. The willow who neither knew the law nor practiced good deeds had little claim to leadership, but in spite of these failings, she had a certain mass appeal.

Again the neutral tree came up with a solution. "Why not," he asked, "combine the palm, the myrtle, and the willow in such a way as to create a new plant and let that plant represent the United Skinny Malinks?" Loud applause followed this suggestion and so the the three plants were joined together and given the new name of lulav.

And so, in the Autumn of a year whose number has been lost in antiquity, the Roly Polies led by the etrog and the Skinny Malinks led by the lulav, marched into the court of the Most High. A hush fell among the plants as Elijah, the court clerk, explained the procedure. The lulav was the first to take the stand.

"Lord Master of the Universe, we humbly thank You for the wonderful world in which You have planted us. Earth, moon, and stars testify to Thy power and certainly we Skinny Malinks recognize its authority. However, there is one little matter which in Your infinite wisdom You might have overlooked. Have You considered the Roly Polies? Have You noticed their gluttony, their gross clamoring for *all* the sunshine, for *all* the rainwater, for *all* the best soil, so that they may grow rounder and rounder still? And it is not alone a matter of our height as contrasted with their abominable width, but where almost all of us are colored nature's own green, they are cursed with skins of all colors. Such hues are an abomination to Thee, O Lord, with their

175

lemon yellows, oranges, reds, browns, and most recently they have actually produced a cauliflower with a skin, colored white! Abomination I cry and so humbly plead that these overstuffed circles be removed from the earth forever.''

Proudly the lulav took his seat amid cheers and boos and the etrog took the stand.

''Holy is Thy name O Lord, the whole earth is full of Thy glory. But can the King of Kings sit idle while the vile Skinny Malinks take over the world? Should not the Lord of Justice do justly? You have heard the words of their mouth, their iniquity is revealed before Thee. Yes, they are green, green with envy and their greenness threatens to smother the earth. Already the green grass is on a rampage and soon we will be completely surrounded by green stalks and clinging vines. Yon lulav has a lean and hungry look. Such plants are dangerous. We Roly Polies are plump with love and our fruits are sweet. The only thing the Skinny Malink is suited for is the manufacture of chlorophyl toothpaste. We therefore propose the total elimination of these pests forever.''

With great majesty, the Lord of Hosts arose. ''My children'' he began, ''you do not understand. I, the Lord am One, and so you must be one, one united plant family. The Skinny Malinks alone, the Roly Polies alone are nothing. Only by working together can you fulfill your higher purpose.''

''We have a higher purpose!'' gasped the Skinny Malinks.

''A higher purpose,'' marveled the Roly Polies.

''Silence in the Court Room!'' thundered Elijah.

"The higher purpose that you serve," continued the Lord, "is man."

"Does he too have a higher purpose?" asked a brash lemon.

The Lord blushed modestly. "Yes, he too has a higher purpose, but *your* higher purpose is to serve man, to offer him materials from which he can make clothing, build shelters, and obtain food. Neither the Skinny Malinks nor the Roly Polies alone can nourish man, but if you work together he can thrive. Now do you understand how foolish your quarrel is in the sight of the Lord?"

"Ahem," said the lulav. "Of course, we did not know of this higher purpose. It changes matters somewhat."

"Certainly," said the etrog. "If we have been entrusted with a higher purpose we must do all we can to fulfill it. The plants of the world must unite for peace."

"Do I have your promise that the plant world will be at peace?" asked the Lord.

"Yes!" shouted the Skinny Malinks.

"Yes!" echoed the Roly Polies.

"I would like a sign," said the Lord, "to seal this covenant. Hereafter in the season of the harvest of the plants, in the time known as Sukkot, the etrog and lulav, as a symbol of the unity of the plant world, will present themselves together to man to serve as his symbol of the holiday of the Harvest."

Rabbi Stanley Yedwab

* * *

177

Mr. Rambunctious Timothy

Far above the village, high up on the hills where the grass was scarce and the roads stony, lived a magnificent ram. His name was Mr. Rambunctious Timothy. His fleece was pure white and on his head glistened two huge marvellous horns which proclaimed his leadership to the world. For Rambunctious Timothy was no ordinary ram, but the respected leader of an entire herd. The sheep loved Rambunctious for the care he took of them and they respected and feared him for his two mighty horns. When Rambunctious wasn't busy chasing a lost lamb or prodding a lazy sheep, he was content to climb to the highest hill from which he could overlook the entire herd. At such times his heart would swell with pleasure and he would, as likely as not, sing his song. If you listen carefully perhaps you can hear him.

> I am a ram, I am
> A great big wonderful ram
> And now that I am grown
> I'm proudest of the horns I own
> For by them you can tell
> I'm a ram, not a lamb.

Yes, life was indeed good. Rambunctious gazed admiringly at his reflection mirrored in a nearby lake and then looked to check his sheep below. Oh, those two sheep were fighting again. Well, one nudge of his horn would end that! And with one backward glance at

178

the lake, Mr. Rambunctious Timothy started off to do his duty.

At the very same time, far below in the village where the people lived, there was a great outcry, there was confusion, and not a little fear. The Jewish townfolk had discovered a great theft. On the Eve, yes, on the very Eve of the Holy Day of Yom Kippur, the sacred Shofar had been stolen from the synagogue.

"Yom Kippur without a Shofar?" cried a little man in a brown suit. "This cannot be. Without the mighty blast of the Shofar there just can not be a Yom Kippur Service."

"No Shofar," wailed his wife, "whatever shall we do?"

"I just don't know." said a second man, not too helpfully. "The stores are already closed, and besides ours was the only Shofar in town."

"That's it, that's it," broke in a third man excitedly. "Ours is the only Shofar in *town,* but have you thought of the hills above the town?"

"Stupid man," said the woman, "there are no people from whom we could borrow a Shofar in those hills. There are only sheep there."

"My dear lady," answered the man, "from people we get only silly talk, from sheep," and here he paused dramatically, "from sheep, we get horns. A male sheep is a ram and a ram has horns. A Shofar is made out of the ram's horn and so, my friends, you need not be a student of Talmud to see that if we go into those hills and find a ram, we will also have found our Shofar."

For the first time since the theft had been discovered,

the villagers allowed themselves to smile.

"Splendid idea," said the first man. "Come, together we shall go into the hills."

The men cheered, but the woman sat and shook her head over the folly of men.

Cautiously the two men climbed among the baby lambs and the sheep until finally they spotted Mr. Rambunctious Timothy himself.

"Rambunctious," they called. Rambunctious turned and drew himself up to his full height. "Mr. Rambunctious Timothy, if you please, sir."

"Oh, er, yes of course. Well then, Mr. Rambunctious Timothy . . ." and with that the man in the brown suit proceeded to tell the ram of the theft, and then explained the importance of the ram's horn to the Yom Kippur Service.

"And so," he concluded timidly, "you can see for yourself how much we would appreciate it if you were to give us one of your horns."

"Give you one of my horns? Give you one of my big beautiful horns?" shouted the ram "Never!" And with that he began to sing his song, but this time angrily.

I am a ram, I am
A great big wonderful ram
And now that I am grown
I'm proudest of the horns I own
For by them you can tell
I'm a ram, not a lamb!

"I will never part with my horns," he concluded.

180

"Indeed I cannot, for only with their help can I lead this fine flock of sheep."

"Oh, but Mr. Ram," pleaded the man in the brown suit. "We ask only for one horn, surely a mighty leader such as yourself could lead the sheep with the remaining horn. And besides, it would be a mitzvah."

"Excuse me sir, but for all my vast knowledge of grass and sheep and seasons, I have no knowledge of what a mitzvah might be. I am not, after all, a Jewish ram."

"A mitzvah," exclaimed the second man, "is a good deed. It is something God wants us to do to help others and thereby to become better people, I mean better sheep, I mean, just better, ourselves."

"And," interrupted the man in the brown suit, "if you donate your horn to this great cause you will be remembered by the Jewish people forever."

"Forever?" asked the ram.

"Forever," repeated the man. "For such a contribution, your sins will be forgiven and your name written in the Book of Life. And the Jewish people will remember you in their prayers, forever!"

"Forever," mused the ram. "Gentlemen, I have decided. I shall give you my horn. I shall do a mitzvah. I shall be remembered by the Jewish people forever!"

And so, dear children, when you hear the sound of the Shofar, as you shall in just one moment, remember Mr. Rambunctious Timothy who gave his most precious possession for the Jewish religion and who wanted so much to be remembered. Remember then this ram, remember his fine sacrifice and consider this, perhaps it

181

is the ram's horn in our Temple that once belonged to Mr. Rambunctious Timothy.

Rabbi Stanley Yedwab

* * *

Bigger'n God

I think you should know that my father is Ben Bauman. Everybody around here knows he's the best cattleman in the country. Dominic is my pal. Sometimes I go to church with him and his sister Juanita. I think you should also know that Dominic is bigger'n me but Juanita isn't. Juanita gets frightened a lot and prays in Spanish, especially when she hears Bruno bark and she doesn't know why. Bruno's my dog. He's big and shaggy and sometimes gets full of porcupine quills and then Manuel, one of the sheep herders, has to pull them out. And all the while Juanita is crying and praying to God or some saint. There are pictures of saints all over the bunkhouse. Juanita says she knows that God will take care of her if she goes to church.

Tomorrow, my folks tell me, I will not see my friends. Instead, I'll have to get dressed up in store clothes and go to Sunday School. My Dad talked to me and said that we're Jews and that Jews don't pray to the

182

saints and that Jesus was a Jew. It doesn't make much sense to me. I asked Dominic about it because he knows all about Jesus but he just scratched his toe in the mud and told me he couldn't tell me 'coz I'd get mad. I told my father what Dominic said and he took me on his knee and looked very sour and glum and said, "Yes, Jesus was a Jew but some people say the Jews killed Jesus. When you're older I'll tell you more about it." That kind of an answer always gets me mad 'coz it isn't an answer at all. Now, I know my father knows everything. But why does he think I'm too dumb to get answers and not too dumb to ride fence with him or to help mix the cattle dip? Of course they watch me doing that 'coz they're scared I might fall in. Dominic and Juanita's parents aren't scared. Mother says they don't want me to hurt myself 'coz they love me. D'ya have to be so darn careful just 'coz people love you? I bet Dominic and Juanita's parents love them too and they're not so careful. Well anyway, I'd rather watch the mountains and the tumble-weed and follow a coyote track (it's alright to do this in the daytime 'coz you won't find the coyote anyway). Sometimes I watch Pablo mix adobe brick for the houses. It doesn't get hard unless you put ox-blood and cattle hair in it. Then it gets good and hard. My father said I have to go to Sunday School to learn what a Jew is. Once I heard a story about Moses. He must have been some kind of a giant. At least that's what he looked like in the picture on the front of the book.

Well here I am at Sunday School. I'm washed and scrubbed. I feel like a piece of dressed beef and the kids on the ranch said that I won't have any fun here. The Sunday School building here in Albuquerque is bigger'n our one-room schoolhouse. The class (that's what they call the bunch of kids sitting in a row in front of the teacher) is all dressed up and I'm a bit scared. When I'm scared I start to sweat. Everyone in the class is looking at me as if I was somethin' funny. The teacher is telling some kind of a story and I don't know half what it's about 'coz I like to look out the window. The teacher (Mr. Cohen is his name) says "Donald, pay attention" in a kind of angry voice.

That makes me more scared and Mr. Cohen knows it. I'm sittin' next to a funny lookin' girl. She's all clean and I wonder what would happen if she fell in a horse trough. (I forgot to tell you that except for Juanita, I don't like girls.)

Mr. Cohen said, "Donald, meet Phyllis Levy."

What am I suppose to do? I'm sittin' next to her so I met her.

She said "Hello, Donald."

And I said "Howdy."

All the time I wondered what she would do if I pinched her. I bet she'd squeal.

Mr. Cohen keeps goin' on saying, "God created heaven and earth."

He created everything, Mr. Cohen says. I poked Phyllis Levy and whispered. "Who's God? Is he the same fella the folks on the ranch pray to?" Ya' know what she said?

She said, "Are you stupid?"

I wanted to sock her one. I hate girls. And all the time

his talk about God doin' this and God doin' that and God making everything. If God is so all-fire good, why did he let Pedro get shot by mistake, and why did the cattle die of loco-weed last year, and why is Aunt Elsie always talking about the people she misses 'coz they're dead? She says they've gone to heaven, but if God is so all-fire good why did He take them to heaven and leave Aunt Elsie here all alone?

"You see, children," says Mr. Cohen, "God is bigger than anything in the world or even out of it. He punishes you when you are bad and rewards you when you are good. He knows everything."

I got to figgerin' he isn't half as good as this guy says 'coz if he was he'd do what my dad does when the cattle are hungry. Feed 'em from an airplane. And when they're sick get the vet. And bring in the Doc for the sick people around the ranch. I'd just about had enough of this God stuff so I raised my hand (that's what you're supposed to do if you want to say something or go to the bathroom). I was madder'an an angry mongoose, and I said, "My Father's bigger'n God."

On the way home I was all mixed up. Isn't it true my father's bigger'n God? My father doesn't hurt people the way God seems to sometimes. But when I said that about my Dad everyone in the class laughed. I'm not goin' to that crazy old school anymore.

When we were riding home on the Sandia Road my father asked me how I liked the school. I told him I didn't like it and also about how mad Mr. Cohen got me. I said to him: "Dad, what's funny about sayin' you're bigger'n God? You're the biggest man I know and nobody's goin' to say any different, not even that schoolteacher.''

My father said he'd tell me all about it later, maybe at bedtime. But then he changed that and said no one could tell anyone all about God 'coz he's so great. Later on I asked Dominic and Juanita if they'd tell me about this guy God and the saints and stuff. Well they told me all kinds of stories about how God loves kids and how he takes people to heaven after they die, and how the saints are good people who were very close to God and talked to Him and prayed and stuff, and how the Buenos Dios is always with us. Even when Injun Joe died from copper-head poisoning, they said, he went to heaven and I'd see him again if I was good. I don't want to die. I'm scared 'coz two days ago I saw a heifer die and that's no fun. They kept tellin' me how wonderful it is in heaven.

If it's so wonderful why don't you all kill yourselves?'' I said. Dominic called me silly and said we couldn't do that 'coz God has given us a job to do on earth. He said even if there were nasty things and hard jobs we should do them as well as we can 'coz that prepares us for heaven. I didn't understand this at all so I decided to go off by myself and play "Geronimo."

At supper time the folks didn't say much about Sunday School and I was glad. Grandpa came for supper and said a Hebrew prayer before we ate. I was wonderin' whether God didn't understand American. I got ready for bed (which in our house means taking a bath and scrubbing your neck and having your ears cleaned). Why I had to go through all that I don't know

186

'coz I just went through the washin' and dressin' bit for Sunday School, and I was only half dirty anyway. I got into bed and my father came in and sat down by me (at first I made believe I was asleep but that didn't work). My father said, "Donald, do you remember when we filled up the gopher holes so that the cattle wouldn't break a leg and the hands wouldn't hurt themselves in the dark?"

I said, "Yeah. What's that got to do with God?"

"Well how do you think the gophers felt about it?"

"Who cares how the gophers felt. They just do harm."

"Do you remember how we had to chase the bobcat out of the corral and how Manuel got an extra bonus for shooting him?"

"Well the bobcat is a heller. Dominic says that the devil's in him."

"I don't think that the devil is in him, Donald. He just wanted something to eat, and how do you think he felt when we shot him?"

I told my father I'm no bobcat thinker.

"Well, he felt pretty bad," my father said, "because he was hungry and we couldn't let him have what he wanted because the cattle belong to us. And besides, if he was around none of us would be safe. But from the bobcat's point of view," Dad said, "we're killers. Do you remember that big red anthill in the aspen grove, Donald? We had to destroy it because the ants, at least that kind of ant, could have gotten into the wooden bunkhouse."

"Well, they're carpenter ants," I said.

"But what about the ants' thinking?" Dad said.

"I'm not an ant thinker."

Then he said, "There are many things that we human beings cannot understand or can only half understand. Maybe the ants thought, when we put a stick in their house and broke it up, that we were some terrible God breaking up their world. Remember, we're too big for an ant to see all of us, and we can't see everything either or we can't understand everything that happens because God is much bigger than we are. Things seem pretty terrible sometimes and then we think of the doctor who saved so many lives last year when there was flu. We believe the doctor was given his skill and his know-how by God. I fell off the horse, and I hurt myself and had to go to Doc Bailey. God doesn't hurt himself and I don't believe he wants to hurt anything else. But we're like the little ants and only see that our little world is being destroyed. Don't forget, Donald, we also don't know how God gives us the brains to do all the good things we do. No matter what we know there's always much more to know. You do what you know to do and I do what I know, but all this is very small compared to what we can know as we get older and learn more. But even then we cannot put the stars where they are or make the sun rise. Let's think of God as someone who knows much more than we know. Whatever we know and can learn and can do is because God has given us just a little bit of his greatness. May God bless you, son."

Before I went to sleep I got to thinking, "Maybe God is bigger'n my Dad."

Rabbi Herbert I. Bloom

* * *

Busy Izzy

Once there was a boy named Isaac. As soon as he began to walk, he used to knock everything off the coffee table, pull books off the shelves, and tear the leaves off the plants. When he grew older, he got worse. He was always on the go. He just could not sit still. He used to run in and out of the house, slamming the door each time. He would turn on the television set and then suddenly dash out of the house without turning it off. He used to run up and down steps, scraping the floor with his heavy play shoes. He just couldn't sit still one moment, and pretty soon it was obvious that Isaac was too dignified a name for him. His father once said, "Goodness, that boy of ours is as busy as a bee." And from that time on, they used to call him "Busy Izzy," and the name stuck, as nicknames do.

Izzy wasn't really a bad boy, just very mischievous. No sooner was he out of school than he would run across the school yard, letting out ear-splitting yells. As soon as he got out of religious school, he would jump around on the grass like a frisky animal.

"Izzy, my son," his mother would plead, "when will you learn to behave like a human being? You are so wild that horns are beginning to grow out of your head."

For a moment Izzy was shocked, but when he put his hands to his head and felt no horns, he was happy again and continued with his pranks.

Then came Rosh Hashanah. Izzy went to temple with his parents and was very excited when in the middle of the service the Shofar was blown. Izzy had never seen a horn like that. It was much better than the police whistle which his father had once brought him, and it seemed more interesting than even the cornet which he studied at school. So, after everybody had left the Temple, Busy Izzy sneaked back and hurried up to the pulpit. He took out the Shofar and gave it a quick blow. A facinating sound came out. He sounded it again and again, and this time the custodian heard it.

"Get out of here, you rascal," he yelled. "Put that Shofar down at once!" Busy Izzy ran away. The custodian picked up the Shofar and put it in the drawer of the pulpit muttering to himself, "that terrible boy."

But Busy Izzy stole back into the temple. He went up to the pulpit and there he found the Shofar in the drawer. Gleefully he put it to his lips, filled his cheeks with air and blew for all he was worth. The sounds came out entirely to Izzy's satisfaction, but the custodian, who was crossing the lawn at the time, heard the sound, and dashed back into the Sanctuary.

"Give me that Shofar, and if you touch it again I shall see that your father gives you the biggest whacking you ever had," said the custodian. He snatched the Shofar out of Izzy's hand and Izzy scampered off.

A few more days went by and the custodian thought he had taught Busy Izzy a lesson for good. But not a bit of it. Izzy couldn't stay good that long, so the following Sunday morning he quietly slipped into the temple when the doors were open. He looked around until he found the Shofar, which this time was hidden in a closet. Izzy really didn't mean to annoy the custodian this time, but the Shofar had such a strange fascination for him that he felt he simply had to try it again.

The urge came upon him to give just a little blow, not a big one. So Izzy put the Shofar to his lips and gave a weak blow. Nothing happened. He took a deep breath and gave a bigger blow. Again nothing happened. He turned the Shofar upside down and blew into the wide end to see if anything had gotten stuck in it. He shook it again, and again put it to his lips. This time Izzy filled his cheeks with a lot of air. His cheeks were puffed out and he looked ready to burst with the tremendous effort he was making, but blow as he would, not a sound came forth, just a husky empty echo of nothing. Well, this got Izzy very mad, and waving the Shofar in front of him he said, "What's the matter with you, you useless horn?"

"Useless, am I?" Busy Izzy eerily discovered that the Shofar was answering him.

"Listen to me, young Isaac," the Shofar continued, "there are a few things you ought to hear."

"I knew another young Isaac long long ago. He was a

191

much finer boy than you. He would not have treated a Shofar like a toy as you did, nor would he have been so disrespectful. In fact, the other Isaac was ready to sacrifice his young life because he and his father believed that anything that God asked them to do should be done. Of course, God did not want him to be sacrificed. God just wanted to know if he was faithful to Him, and so God sent a ram to be sacrificed in place of Isaac. And here is where we come to the Shofar made of a ram's horn, my young friend.''

"Golly, I'm beginning to see how badly I've behaved," said Busy Izzy quickly. "I'm really ashamed of myself. I'm sorry I insulted you.''

"Another thing, Isaac,'' continued the Shofar. "You'd imagine that God could have chosen a finer and more musical instrument to use as a Shofar, wouldn't you? Something like a clarinet or a saxophone or a cornet. But no, God does everything with a purpose, and His purpose in choosing a ram's horn to be blown on this holy day is to make the Jewish people, and especially Jewish boys and girls, stop and wonder. God wants them to think about how they have acted and how they have behaved, and to see in what way they are superior to animals. Sure, an animal also eats and sleeps and runs around wild and makes noises, but a human being must look after his conduct, behave himself, and show that he is more than just a wild animal. I am only a ram's horn, but when I am blown on Rosh Hashanah and Yom Kippur, I remind all that you should be sorry for the bad things and urge you to do better.''

"Say, that's real neat,'' said Izzy. "I never looked at

it that way before. I will really try to improve, I promise," he said eagerly.

"And let me tell you something else, young fellow," said the Shofar. "You say that I am helpless and useless. Did you know that when the Jewish people were called together at Mount Sinai to receive the Ten Commandments, it was I who called them together? First I called the children together with a nice strong sound, a Tekiah. Then I called the fathers and mothers together with the Shevarim. And then I called the old people together with a Teruah. And when they were assembled, God was ready to give them the Ten Commandments."

"Boy, you really are important," said Izzy.

"And another thing, when the Jewish people were wandering in the desert they grew tired. They did not want to continue their journey, just to fall asleep and not go to the land that God had promised them. Then again I blew a sound. I woke them all up. They gathered up their tents and their possessions and they marched forward again."

"You mean like an alarm clock?" said Izzy.

"Better than an alarm clock," answered the Shofar, "because they couldn't shut me off when I began to sound. I wouldn't let them rest until they started going forward."

"Well, what happened to you then?" asked Izzy.

"After the Jewish people got into Palestine and began to live according to the way God taught them, they used me for special occasions. Every seven years there was the Year of Jubilee. Then everyone would rest. They let

193

the earth rest too. Slaves were freed. I used to get up on a mountain top and call out to everybody that freedom was to rule over the entire country."

"Say, that's something like that school bell of ours," said Izzy. "As soon as I hear that ring in the afternoon I also am free."

"And that's not all," continued the Shofar. "After the Jews had left Palestine and were living in countries all over the world, they used to be busy trying to make a living, but some bad people did not treat the Jews well. Some Jews lost hope. But every year on the Holy Days they would hear the Shofar. They gained new hope."

"I'm sorry that I called you useless and helpless," said Busy Izzy with tears in his eyes.

The temple was silent as Izzy left it.

When he came home he softly opened up the door and closed it carefully. He walked quietly into the kitchen where his mother was preparing dinner. Going up to her, he put his arms around her, pulled her head down to his and kissed her.

"What is this?" said his mother. "You can't be my lovable Busy Izzy. You came into the house like an angel."

"Well, mom, I think I'm going to try to act like an angel from now on," said Izzy. "Can I help you with anything?"

"No thanks, Izzy. I don't need any help right now," replied his mother.

"Well, I'm going upstairs to wash my face and hands and do my homework and study my Sunday School lessons before dinner time," said Izzy.

"Aren't you going to turn on the television?" asked his mother.

"No," said Izzy. "I've heard so many wonderful stories today that nothing can beat them. And by the way, Mom," he called back as he started to walk upstairs, "would you mind not calling me Busy Izzy anymore. I like the name you gave me when I was born. Just call me Isaac."

And with that he walked upstairs quietly and his mother heard him turn on the water to wash, and then go to his room to pick up some clothes which he had scattered around on the floor. She turned back to the stove where she was cooking dinner, and with a smile on her lips she wiped a tear from her eye and said, "Thank heaven!"

Rabbi Julius J. Nodel

* * *

How To Be Sorry

Each of our Holy Days gives us a chance to say something to God that is important. On Sukkot, the Feast of Booths, we say "thank you" to God for giving us the fruits of the earth to help us grow strong and healthy. On Pesach, the Feast of Passover, we remember that our ancestors were slaves in Egypt and we resolve to try to help all men to be free. On Chanukah, the Feast of Dedication, we remember the Maccabees and we say, "We will be strong and courageous." Today is Yom Kippur, the Day of Atonement, and we say two important words on this holiest day of the year. We try to say, "I'm sorry."

We all try to be good boys and girls during the year, but there are times when we make mistakes. There are times when we are not as helpful as we should be; times when we don't do what we are told to do; times when we give our parents more trouble than we should. Usually, when we do something wrong we do say, "I'm sorry." I think there must be some of us here who do not come when we are first called and who are late for dinner. There must be some of us here who do not hang up our clothes and who leave our rooms in a mess. I think there must be some of us here who are not always kind to little brothers or sisters. Some of us do not always share our games with friends. These are the mistakes we make and the only way we can become better people is to be able to say, when we have done something wrong, "I'm sorry. I'll try not to do it again."

There is much more to it than that, though. Just saying you are sorry isn't really being sorry. How do you know that a person really is sorry? Well, first of all, he really doesn't do it again. And second, and much more important, he tries to do something nice and kind in place of the wrong thing he has just done. If you spill the milk all over your mother's good tablecloth, it just isn't enough to say, "I'm sorry," nor is it enough just to help clean up the milk because that is just making the

196

mistake disappear. What is important is that you do a little something extra to show that you really regret what you did. Wouldn't it be a good idea if you asked your mother if you could polish the table and make it shine brightly, so that you would turn your mistake into a shiny, bright good deed? It just isn't enough to say, "I'm sorry," when you've gotten into an argument and have lost your temper and perhaps hit someone. You have to do something good in return, maybe give him a little present or invite him to your house to play. Then you show him you really are sorry and you turn someone you thought was an enemy into a friend.

Let me tell you a story that really isn't true, but that shows how this procedure of being sorry works. You all know of King Solomon, and how wise and kind he was. But did you know that he could talk the language of animals and that birds and fish and insects used to bring their problems to him? The story says that on every Rosh Hashanah he used to call all the living things in his kingdom to his palace and wish them a Happy New Year. They would stay for Yom Kippur and have services, too.

One year, King Solomon was sitting on his throne, surrounded by all the creatures of his animal kingdom, and wishing them a Happy New Year. Way back in the great crowd was a swarm of bees that had flown all the way from their mountain hive to be at the great occasion. Thousands and thousands of bees were sitting in the section reserved for them. Among them was one bright little bee who had come for the first time. She was as thrilled as she possibly could be. How handsome

197

King Solomon looked to her! What she liked most about him was his nose. He had a beautiful nose and she had a very strong urge to go up and sting King Solomon on that beautiful nose of his. Now I think we would all agree that this was a wrong thing to do; even if we do have urges to do things that are wrong, we should know better. However, this was a very young bee and the nose looked so attractive that she left her seat in the bees' section, and buzzing all along the way, made a beeline straight to King Solomon's nose. Before the king knew what had happened to him he was stung right on his left nostril. He reached out and grabbed the little bee in his hand and said to her, "How dare you sting the king!" The little bee replied, "Oh, Your Majesty, I'm sorry. I know it was wrong, but I just couldn't resist." The king asked, "Are you really sorry?" and the little bee said, "Yes, I am really sorry. I won't do it again." King Solomon said, "Very well. If you are really sorry I will forgive you," and he let the little bee go. She fluttered back to her mother and father in the bees' section. They were very angry and hoped their child would improve her manners.

About three weeks later King Solomon received a message that the Queen of Sheba was going to pay him a visit. The queen, who had heard about King Solomon's wisdom, thought she was very smart, too. So, when she came to the court she decided to test his wisdom. She brought three questions which she planned to ask him. When she bowed low before his throne, she said, "O great King, I understand you are the wisest person in the world. I have come to test you. If you are able to answer my three questions then, indeed, I shall agree that you are wise; but if you do not know the answers I shall proclaim throughout the world that the Queen of Sheba is wiser than King Solomon." And the king said, "Very well. Ask your questions."

"My first question," said the queen, "is this: What is the most valuable substance in the whole world?" King Solomon, without pausing even for a moment, said, "So teach us to number our days that we may get us a heart of wisdom, for wisdom is more precious than rubies and knowledge is better than much fine gold." The queen was amazed, but realized it was true. We can lose rubies and gold but the wisdom and learning we have in our minds can never be lost.

The queen's next question was a little more difficult. She asked King Solomon, "What is the finest meal a man can eat?" Again, without pausing, the king said, "Better by far is a meal of the simplest food if it is served with love, than a meal of the finest food served with hate."

Well, the Queen of Sheba realized that the king was really wise in the ways of men. She clapped her hands, whereupon two men entered, each carrying a beautiful rose. They stood before King Solomon, and the queen said, "O wise King, one of these roses is real; the other was made with the greatest skill by one of my artists. Without touching or smelling them can you tell me which is the real rose?" This was indeed the greatest test. The king looked at the roses. He looked from one rose to the other, but each was so perfect he could not make up his mind. And then, suddenly, through one of the open palace windows a little dot flew, buzzing. It buzzed around the room two or three times, then flew straight to one of the roses and started to sip its nectar. Immediately, King Solomon pointed to that rose and said, "The one on the left is the real rose. The other is artificial." Whereupon the queen said, "King Solomon, everything I have heard is true. You are indeed the wisest man in all the world." She left him precious gifts and went back to Sheba, satisfied that King Solomon was indeed great in wisdom.

No sooner had she left, the king summoned the little bee and said, "Thank you, my precious creature." The little bee said, "Perhaps you do not remember me, sire, but it was I who last Rosh Hashanah stung you on your nose. I said that I was sorry but I have been waiting all this time to prove to you in some way that I was really sorry. I know that words themselves don't really mean I am sorry." The king said, "Dear bee, you indeed have learned wisdom, for a person can only show that he is truly sorry by doing a good deed to the person he has hurt." So King Solomon blessed the bee and she returned happily to her home.

So we see that saying "I'm sorry" is the first step to becoming better people. We pray to God today and tell Him we are sorry for all of our mistakes. Let us add to our prayers the happy thought that we will show how sorry we are by being considerate and kind and by making our mistakes over into good and kind deeds. This is the wisdom which this day gives to us. If we learn it well then we, too, shall receive the blessing of our parents, our teachers, and our friends. But, moreover, we can imagine that the wise King Solomon would also be proud of us, and that the little bee would give us her blessing, too.

Rabbi Solomon K. Kaplan

* * *

Name and Profession, Please

The regiment stood stiffly at attention as the general reviewed the disciplined troops. Suddenly, the general stopped in his tracks and called out, "Is there a tailor in the regiment?"

A bright young soldier nearby eagerly raised his hand, saying, "I am a Taylor, sir."

The general motioned the perplexed soldier to follow him to the barracks. "Young man," said the general as soon as the door was closed, "a seam in my jacket came apart on the review field. Please sew it for me."

"I don't know how to sew," said the troubled soldier. The general managed a smile as he reminded him that he had answered the call for a tailor. "But sir," apologized the soldier, "I am not a tailor by profession; my name is Taylor."

How tragically reminiscent of this story is the plight of the person who is Jewish in name only. He carries with him a badge, the responsibilities of which he does not recognize, the beauties of which he cannot appreciate, the celestial message of which he fails to grasp.

It is no more than a heavy burden to bear with stoic resignation an enigmatic name to defend against its many deprecators. How enviable by contrast is the lot of the person who is a Jew in name and in deed.

Rabbi Victor Solomon

* * *

Source of Power

The eerie music of the wailing siren roused me from a deep, refreshing sleep. It was close to midnight. Could this be an air-raid warning, or something else? I decided to check with the radio. Half awake, I reached for the radio and turned it on. Five minutes passed—why does the radio fail to go on? Oh, I know! The dial must be set between stations. I turned the station-selector. Still no sound. I turned the knob to "loudest." Dead!

Something must be wrong with the radio; a tube or something must have gone bad. The time has come to throw the set out and buy a new one! I turned on the light to check, and chuckled as the riddle was solved: There was nothing wrong with the radio. It just was not plugged in!

202

How many people lay the blame for their woes at the feet of religion. They "believe" in God but He has let them down! They pray but get no answer. Anxiously, they turn to their spiritual radio in the darkness of despair. They turn all the knobs with trembling fingers; and when the signal does not come through they condemn the instrument and discard it.

A little light and a lot of humility would place the blame where it belongs, at their own doorstep. Sure they manipulate the knobs correctly and listen attentively to a perfect instrument. But nothing comes through because they have neglected to connect it with the Source of Power.

Rabbi Victor Solomon

* * *

When Grief Comes

There is nothing wrong with weeping. It is a natural emotional safety valve. Sometimes you even weep when a dear friend leaves on a train or boat for a few weeks of vacation. How much deeper is the wound and how much greater the pain when you must say good-bye to a loved one for the last time. But God gives comfort to those who turn to Him with faith.

There is nothing wrong with grief. It is a natural

expression of a bereaved human soul. But do not weep to yourself. Turn to God for consolation. Share your joy with others. Save your sorrow for God. Share it with Him. Do not refuse to be comforted. After the first tears of grief, sorrow becomes a matter of faith.

The sensitive person will find even in grief a means of personality development and self-improvement. A doctor deeply loved his baby daughter. She was an only child. One day she fell ill and nothing could save her. When she died, the broken father observed the traditional mourning period and then, went out to keep others babies from dying.

Grief can bring greater refinement of character and deeper understanding of the suffering and needs of others. It has the power to bestow upon you the gift of empathy and to make you a better person for the experience.

May God protect us from sorrow. But when grief comes, turn to God. He will not fail you in your hour of need.

Rabbi Victor Solomon

* * *

Close at Hand

One of my congregants came to me with a dream. She dreamed that she was standing all alone in front of a thick glass window. She saw God on the other side. With hope, and overcome with emotion, she began to knock on the glass to attract His attention. Suddenly, she heard a sweet voice beside her asking, "Why are you making so much noise?" Then she realized that God had been near her all the time, and that what she believed she saw on the other side was only a reflection of what was really close at hand.

Most of us go through life looking for God in the "other room." An unhappy feeling of estrangement from divine guidance and spiritual experience haunts us and makes life empty of meaning. Spiritual grandeur and limitless hope are the things we see beyond the thick glass. Happiness is there too, but who can penetrate the shatterproof wall of glass whose lucid transparency only adds the woes of Tantalus to the pains of loneliness?

But those who will but listen will hear a still, sweet voice. It tells us that the blissful living which seems beyond our reach is but a reflection of God's bountiful gifts surrounding us, which can be ours for the asking.

Rabbi Victor Solomon

*   *   *

The Little Things

The inimitable Henry Ward Beecher once illustrated the need for tact in conjunction with truth in his story of a self-conscious young woman who went to a store to purchase a pair of shoes. After measuring her feet the salesman exclaimed: "Lady, one of your feet is bigger than the other!" Frightened, she ran out of the store and into the open door of another shoe store. The second salesman politely asked her to sit down and proceeded to measure her feet for a new pair of shoes. "My dear," he said gently after he had taken the measurement, "one of your feet is smaller than the other." The young lady was very pleased and left the store with two pairs of shoes.

In our daily living we come into contact with many people. We deal with husband, wife, child, parent, teacher, pupil, friend, neighbor, and a host of human beings upon whom we exercise a profound influence through word and deed. We affect their lives not only by the content of what we say, but often by the way in which we say it.

The smile which accompanies a "good morning," the warmth of a handshake, the genial tone of a word of encouragement go a long way in making life more pleasant, and social living more enjoyable for all concerned.

These are the "little things" in life which often escape us in a fast-moving world of "big events." But when liberally used they could become the "great things" in life, changing a drab and dreary existence into triumphant living.

This is the Jewish way of life.

Rabbi Victor Solomon

* * *

Seeing the Unseen

"If I from my spy-hole," wrote Robert Louis Stevenson, "looking upon a fraction of the universe, yet perceive some broken evidences of a plan, shall I be so mad as to complain that all cannot be deciphered?" Mortal man, unheedful of his limitations strives to see all and to know all. This is impossible. The unhappiest of men is he who rejects all faith because of his frustrated attempt to see the unseen.

Yet, the unseen may be seen by a man of faith. Spiritual horizons widen and new dimensions of the soul manifest themselves to the person who is in search of Truth through Faith.

An artist once lectured on the beauty of a sunset. He went into ecstasy as he described this infinite expression of nature in a divine array of colors and color combinations. But he could not help but notice a young man in the audience who did not seem to share his enthusiasm.

207

Throughout the talk, this man wore a look of skepticism and unconcealed contempt on his face. He was color blind. After the lecture he came up to the artist and said: "Sir, you gave a wonderful talk, but I am sorry to say that I did not see the beautiful colors which you tried to describe." The artist sadly looked at him and said: "But don't you wish you could?"

Color blindness is an innocent freak of nature. But insensitivity to faith is the result of poor habits of thinking and living. It is the disease of the person who relies too much on his own powers and tries to see and understand everything before he is able to understand himself and his own needs. Before we attempt to see the unseen, we must make certain that the veil of spiritual blindness has been lifted from our own eyes.

Rabbi Victor Solomon

* * *

Money Madness

Do you control money, or does money control you? Even so-called religious people can suffer from the affliction of money madness. The motives behind this disease are sundry but the underlying cause is usually psychological. Above all else, the "patient" who is under the intoxicating influence of the dollar sign is to be pitied. He who abandons the Bible book for the bank book has turned stock-market statistics into barometers of false happiness and blinding delusions of security. Like the alcoholic, he loses all self-control and progressively sinks from one level of despair to another. This is the lot of the unfortunate man who permits money to become his master.

To a person of faith, however, money means infinitely more than a means of self-gratification. It means responsibility and a divinely ordained obligation to do good. Money can be used to help the less fortunate, the poor, the sick, and the weak. It can help build schools, houses of worship, and hospitals. When we realize with humility that God is the source of all we have, money begins to assume true spiritual significance.

There is nothing wrong with wealth when it is made to serve man rather than to lord over him. But this happy situation can arise only when our personal economics rest on a strong faith in God as the Giver of all, the Helper of all, and the Redeemer of all.

Rabbi Victor Solomon

*　*　*

The Door

A medieval legend tells the tragic story of a political prisoner in the dungeon of his enemy's castle. The frustration of imprisonment was unbearable. But as the weeks turned into months and the months became years, the poor soul adjusted to the wretched existence which a cruel fate had decreed for him. For twenty lonely years he rotted in his cell. He never saw anyone. Even the guard, who pushed the prisoner's food into the cell through a small opening at the bottom of the door, remained anonymous. One day, the aged prisoner was pacing the cold stone floor of his cell absorbed in thought, when he stopped at the door and absentmindedly turned the knob. There was a loud squeaking of ancient hinges as the huge door slowly opened before the startled man. "My heavens," thought the prisoner, "the door has been unlocked all the time and I never had the sense to try it."

How true this rings for many of us today. We are prisoners of fear and hate and lust. Trapped in cells of our own making we waste valuable days and years of frustration and spiritual atrophy. Yet, we need but try the knob to enter into freedom. Freedom beckons from without. A little bit of faith can do it. Is this what is meant by "freedom of religion?"

Rabbi Victor Solomon

* * *

210

What Is Your Name?

This question appears to be a simple one. Each of us has his name clearly indicated on the official record card in the files.

But as a matter of fact, everyone has more than one name. As a great Jewish teacher of many generations ago put it, "Every person has three names, one which his parents give him at birth, a second given him by the people among whom he lives, and a third which God ascribes to him in the Book of Destiny."

We have no choice about the name which our parents give to us at birth, but we do have control over the name, the reputation, we have among our fellowmen, and the name which God will ascribe to us.

Let each of us help make our community a better place in which to live, so that our real name shall be fine and noble and admired by all.

Rabbi Jesse J. Finkle

* * *

The Man Who Slew the Giant

One of the most popular stories in the Bible is one of David's victory over Goliath. As we go through life, all of us are faced with situations where the odds are against us.

We face "giants" from the time we are little to old age. Perhaps the story of David's triumph is admired because we like to project ourselves into his position. Like him, we want to kill our "giants" and we can, provided we follow his method.

We are all familiar with his victory but we are not equally aware of the means he used to achieve it. David carried five stones in his bag but with them he carried in his heart five qualities of victory.

In the first place, he had courage. He volunteered to fight the giant. He faced up to the challenge which came to him. He met the issue without dodging or ducking.

Second, he had the wisdom not to burden himself with heavy armor. He refused to wear the king's apparel because he had not tested it. In our combat with the "giants" who confront us, we so often take refuge in hand-me-downs, another person's ideas or beliefs, rather than in those resources we have made our own.

Third, David saw to it that he had extra resources. He prepared a margin of safety by choosing five stones from the brook, although only one was necessary. He kept 80 percent of his strength in reserve.

In the fourth place, David met the giant's taunts with a confidence which sprang from an earnest faith in God.

Finally, as the giant lay stunned from the impact of the sling stone, David took Goliath's own sword and slew him. He had the will to use the weapon of the enemy to gain his victory.

David slew the giant because he was a man who had

courage. He had wisdom gained from the experience of the past, he was careful to be well-prepared, he kept an unruffled faith in God under provocation, and he had the wit and ingenuity to turn his enemy's sword against him.

We can also conquer giants if we provide ourselves with these same fine qualities.

Rabbi Jesse J. Finkle

* * *

Busy Here and There

In the days of King Ahab, one of the prophets related a parable: "Thy servants went out into the midst of the battle; and behold a man turned aside and brought a man unto me and said, 'Keep this man; if by any means he be missing, then shall thy life be for his life, or else thou shalt pay a talent of silver.' And as thy servant was busy here and there, he was gone."

In this brief story, we find the picture of what so many people do with their lives. There are some who willfully go about to do evil, but most of us do wrong or fail to do right because we are "busy here and there," doing less important things.

The soldier in the story was no doubt busy with what he considered necessary duties, such as setting his tent

213

in order or polishing his armor for inspection. But while occupied with these things, he neglected the more important duty that was given to him—to guard a captive—and had to pay for this mistake with his life, or a great fine.

So it is with so many people and children as well. We fill up our time and use our energy with many things that we consider to be of value, but our choice is often lopsided and we crowd out of our lives interests which actually are more important to our welfare.

Two things we should remember about the finer aims in life. First, they do not go after us, we must go after them. Such fine things as good books, good music, Sunday School, Hebrew School, and temple attendance don't attract us as much as do exciting comic books, movies, radio, or T.V. programs.

The second thing to remember is that we need these finer objectives in life now, in our childhood days, if we are to live our lives at the highest level and establish a firm foundation for our future. The great treasures of life cannot be put aside like government bonds in a safe-deposit box, where we can be sure to find them when we need them. The great treasures in life are like a campfire; if it is not tended, it will go out. Unless we exercise good habits, we will become weak and spiritually worthless.

Rabbi Jesse J. Finkle

* * *

214

The Story of King David's Cave

According to legend, King David didn't really die. He's only asleep in a mysterious cave, waiting for someone to come and wake him so that he can go forth and lead his people in battle against its foes. Once there were two Jewish students who heard this legend and they determined to go forth in search of the mysterious cave. After traveling many days and inquiring of many wise old men about the cave, they sat down to rest under a big tree. They saw a dove on one of the branches and asked:

Little dove, pretty dove, tell us dear,
Is the cave of King David anywhere near?

The little dove called out: "I cannot tell, but you will get some information from the great river."

So the boys traveled onward many more days and came to the great river, and they cried out, "River, river, tell us, O river, can we the cave of King David discover?" "No, I cannot tell," replied the river, "but travel further and go to the mountain and there you will find the right way."

So they traveled many more days and were about to give up when they came to the mountain and found a cave near the foot of the mountain. As they were about to enter the cave an old man appeared and the boys greeted him with "Shalom Aleichem." "Aleichem Shalom," replied the old man. "Go forward into the cave and fear nothing. You will come upon a big stone

215

blocking the way—roll it out of your path and you will find what you are seeking, the secret chamber of King David. But you must remember this one thing: as soon as the King stretches out his hands, you must grab the pitcher of water you will find near his bed and pour the water over his hands. Then you will see marvelous things—King David will rise from his long sleep, and he will go forth to gather all the children of Israel now scattered in exile, and bring them back to the holy city of Jerusalem.''

As soon as he finished speaking, the old man was swept up into heaven by a flaming chariot, and the boys then knew that he was the prophet Elijah. With pounding hearts they entered the cave. They came upon the big stone which they pushed aside, and then entered the room where King David was sleeping. The whole room was lined with bright shining gems and glittered with panels of gold. The scene was so impressive that the boys could hardly breathe.

Then King David stretched out his hands toward them, but they did not notice it because they were still admiring the beautiful gems. They completely forgot what Elijah had told them and did not pour the water over King David's hands. And so, King David dropped his hands beside himself. At that moment the boys remembered what they were told to do, but it was too late. Before they knew it, in a moment they were back home where they started from and the whole experience was for naught!

Rabbi Jesse J. Finkle

* * *

216

Another Opportunity

In the land of Arabia there is a magic mountain about which an interesting story is told. On top of the mountain there was a treasure which was to belong to anyone who could succeed in climbing to it. The difficulty was that anyone climbing up who looked back immediately turned to stone, and many indeed were the stone images along the mountain slope. At last, three brothers decided to climb up and secure the treasure. The eldest brother started first, but soon, he began to hear voices coming from all directions. One threatened him with death if he continued his climbing. Another said he was foolish to imagine that he could accomplish what no one else had done. But still he kept on. Then a voice challenged him by calling him a coward; this was more than he could stand. He turned around to see who it was who insulted him, and at once he turned to stone.

His younger brother did a little better. He managed to climb half way to the top. But soon he too heard voices about him. One sweet voice invited him to rest, and without thinking, he turned around, and was also turned into stone.

When the third brother began to climb he first stopped his ears so that he could not hear anything. When the voices tried to attract his attention, they had no effect at all on him. By persistent effort and by concentrating on his goal, he succeeded in reaching the top of the mountain and gained the treasure that was waiting for him.

217

This story teaches us the secret of a happy life. There are always voices, sweet and attractive, whispering to us, but we must be brave enough to stop up our ears to anything that would lead us from the path of the right and good.

Rabbi Jesse J. Finkle

* * *

Watch Out for Low Ceilings

There was once an old home which appeared very spacious on the outside, but the rooms inside it had very low ceilings. One day when it became necessary to do some repair work on the ceilings, it was discovered that they were not part of the original building. The low ceiling had been added by later generations for so-called "practical" reasons.

Unfortunately, many people's lives are much in the same "fix." Every human being is born with that upward-reaching, beautifully creative impulse of the Divine. Yet how many of us foolishly build in our lives under "lower ceilings"?

Just as it is unsafe for an airplane to take off under weather conditions of a low ceiling, so is it unwise to live under a "low ceiling" of low moral values. It takes courage and conviction to turn away from ungodly standards of living and choose only those activities and interests that will allow our inner beings to soar upward into the glorious realms of spiritual beauty. Make this motto your guide for daily living—watch out for low ceilings!

Rabbi Jesse J. Finkle

* * *

Dress Up on the Inside Too

The story is told of a great Jewish teacher of generations ago who was very homely. One day the Emperor's daughter chided him and said, "What an ugly vessel to contain so much wisdom."

The scholar asked her, "Please tell me, in what kind of vessels do you keep your wine?" "In earthen jars, to be sure," she replied. The scholar then asked: "Should not a princess keep wine in vessels of silver and gold, and not plain earthenware jars?"

The princess took this advice and had the wine transferred to vessels of silver and gold. However, in a short time the wine turned sour. The princess complained to the scholar, and he said: "I just wanted to teach you a lesson, that you should not judge values by outward appearances only. Just as wine keeps best in plain containers, even so is it often with wisdom and character!''

Rabbi Jesse J. Finkle

* * *

There's Enough for Everybody

The story is told that a certain merchant one day came to his rabbi with the complaint that a competitor was going to establish a shop just a short distance away. "For many years," he said, "I have been making a respectable living in my little store, but now I am afraid I may lose out!"

The rabbi thought the matter over and then said to the merchant: "Did it ever occur to you to ask just why, when a horse drinks from a river, he always strikes the water with his hoof? It's because the horse sees his reflection in the river and suspects that it is another horse who has come to deprive him of his water, and so he tries to drive this imaginary horse away. This horse does not realize that there is enough water in the river for himself and others as well!"

"And now, my good man," concluded the rabbi, "a human being must not act like a horse. He must realize that God is good to all his children and has created the world to provide sustenance for them all.''

This story should remind us that abundant opportunities are available to each and every one of us to develop our physical, mental, and spiritual qualities. Remember, there's enough for everybody. Be sure to take the necessary interest and make the necessary effort to get your share!

Rabbi Jesse J. Finkle

* * *

Appreciating What Others Do for Us

The story is told of a certain very pious rabbi who, in his travels, happened to stay at an inn in a small town. Those who served him meals noted that he washed only his fingers, and not the entire hand, before coming to the table. The rabbi was asked: ''Why do you use so little water and wash only your fingers before eating your meals?''

''I'll tell you why,'' replied the rabbi, ''shortly after arriving here, I happened to notice how you obtained your water supply. I saw your servant climbing up the hill weighed down with heavy pails of water drawn from the spring down in the valley. Now, while it is indeed meritorious to wash one's entire hands before meals, we should be considerate of the servant who brings us the

221

water so laboriously. Therefore, it is sufficient to wash only fingers before meals here and thus help conserve the water supply and spare the servant.''

In our own daily living, so few of us stop to realize and appreciate the work and labor performed by others for our benefit! The truly religious individual does not wait to be thanked for his efforts, but those whom he benefits certainly should be considerate of his labors and not use them wastefully!

Rabbi Jesse J. Finkle

* * *

Be Sure to Aim at the Right Target

Many generations ago there lived a great Jewish teacher by the name of Rabbi Meir. One day he complained to his wife Beruriah about how annoying it was to see so many individuals openly ignore religious practices. In his anger he asked God to destroy the callous ones.

But his wife replied that the truly religious pray not that sinners may perish, but that sins may disappear. By a slight change in the original Hebrew of verse 35 of Psalm 104, we are taught to understand not, ''Let the *sinners* be consumed out of the earth so that the wicked will be no more!'' but rather "Let the sins be consumed out of the earth so that the wicked will be no more.'' We should strive to remember this significant teaching in our own generation. We must realize that in democracy's struggle against communism and fascism, we are not only fighting men, we are struggling against evil ideas and ideals which have gripped those who challenge us on the battlefield. This struggle must be carried on within our own ranks as well, as we hopefully look forward to the day when, "Sin shall at last be consumed out of the earth so that the wicked will be no more!''

Rabbi Jesse J. Finkle

* * *

How Far Can You See?

At first glance, this question seems to refer to eyesight. However, it can also be considered in terms of our inner spiritual vision and understanding of the meaning of life. It is related that when the natives of the interior of Africa are asked, "Where does your great river Congo go?'' they reply, "It is lost in the sands of the desert.'' These natives have never seen or heard about the sea to which the Congo surely and irresistibly makes its way. Similarly, when we are discouraged and ask ourselves, "Where do all our labor and effort go?" We are inclined to accept the hopeless answer, "It is all lost." But the truly religious individual looks beyond the immediate present and has the uplifing assurance that worthy labor is not lost or made void, but merges with the divine power of righteousness, which assuredly is destined, some day, to reign supreme in the minds and hearts of men. If we can see this far, ours will be the conviction that corruption is not an irremovable aspect of civilization, that violence and wars are not inevitable among nations, and that mankind is not forever bound to the bloody wheels of the devilish chariots of war and race hatred, prejudice, and bigotry! Inspired by such a faith, we will be impelled to strive in our daily living to help, in our own way, to bring this hope into reality.

Rabbi Jesse J. Finkle

* * *

The Three Vases

The legend is told of a wise king of ancient days who one day invited his three sons to select one of three vases set up before his throne. One of gold, was covered with jewels; the word "Empire" was written on it. The

224

second vase was amber, and had on it the word "Glory." The third vase was made of clay and had no inscription on it.

The eldest son grasped the "Empire" vase, and when he opened it, he saw that it was full of blood. The second son took the "Glory" vase and opened it to behold the ashes of dead heroes. The youngest son took what was left, the vase of clay, and when he opened it, he found therein God's holy name!

The king asked his couriers, "Which vase weighed the most?" "The golden vase of Might," declared the warriors; "The amber vase of Fame," replied the poets; "The clay emblem of Right," cried out the sages.

"O my people," said the king, "remember well the meaning of this lesson, that of all the values, we must learn to cherish above all the name of God, and to shape our lives in accordance with His will!"

We of this generation should pay heed to the meaning of this legend. Let us resolve zealously to pursue as a nation and as individuals, not the "Golden vase of Might," nor the "Amber vase of fame," but the simple "vase of Right."

Rabbi Jesse J. Finkle

* * *

Reaching

The story is told that the people of a certain land, one day saw a most unusual and beautiful bird come and make its nest on top of the tallest tree. When the king heard about it, he issued an order that the bird and its nest be brought down from the top of the tree by means of a human ladder.

As the human ladder was being formed with men standing on each other's shoulders, those who stood nearest to the ground became impatient. Before the ladder was completed, they shook themselves free, so that the project completely collapsed, and the beautiful bird and its nest remained out of reach.

I like to think of this parable as a reminder to each and everyone of us that if mankind is ever to reach the "beautiful bird" of peace and harmony, every member of society must help to build and maintain the human ladder of kindness, friendliness, and helpfulness.

Yes, every single one of us, regardless of our race, religion, wisdom, or strength, constitutes a vital and essential link in the human ladder which must be built and maintained if mankind is to reach and enjoy the "beautiful bird."

Rabbi Jesse J. Finkle

* * *

Very Timely

The story is told of a great scholar who, while traveling, stopped to ask a night's lodging at the home of a rich man. The man didn't take the trouble to find out the traveler's identity, but noticing his dusty clothes assumed he was a vagrant. "Away with you, before I call my servants to come and throw you out," he cried. The sage sadly went away and found lodging with one of the poor families in town. It wasn't long before it became known that this traveler was a great scholar, and soon, the rich man came to beg forgiveness, saying, "I should have asked you who you were and I would have indeed been honored to have you as my guest." "No," replied the sage, "I'm glad you didn't ask me who I was! You should learn to do good to others not by reason of their being important, but because they are fellow human beings!" "Let me give you an example from Scriptures," continued the wise man. "Do you remember the difference between Abraham and Lot? When Abraham ran forth to welcome the three Divine wayfarers, we read, 'And he lifted up his eyes and lo, three *men* stood over against him'; but with Lot we are told . . 'And the *angels* came to Sodom and Lot saw them and rose up to meet them.' Abraham didn't look for angels, only for men to serve, while Lot first looked for angels before he rose up to be of service."

This story reminds us of a basic principle of genuine religion, to deal with our fellowmen for what they are. Let us strive to live each day by this lofty maxim: "I shall pass through this world but once. Any good therefore, that I can do, or any kindness that I can show, to any human being, let me do it now, let me not defer it or neglect it, for I shall not pass this way again."

Rabbi Jesse J. Finkle

* * *

Balanced Diet

In the days of Shakespeare, a certain type of wooden bowl was used at mealtime. The top of the bowl was hollowed out deeply enough to contain the main dish. The bottom, or stand, was only slightly hollowed out in the opposite direction, so that when the main dish was eaten, you simply turned the bowl over and you were served the dessert in the bottom part.

This was done not only to save on bowls and on washing them, but also as a method of disciplining the youngsters, for if they didn't eat all of the main dish, they couldn't get their dessert.

Well, life at its best is very much like this kind of wooden bowl. We should not eat our dessert until we have finished our meat and vegetables. But far too many among us are eating only the "dessert" without tasting too much of the "main dish." We pass up those interests which are meant to develop, train and discipline our character, and eagerly reach out for those interests which are more palatable and enjoyable, but which give us very little, if any, spiritual nourishment and strength.

All of us have to be reminded from time to time that an unbalanced diet in the realm of religious and cultural interests is just as unhealthy and undesirable as an unbalanced diet in the actual food we eat.

Let us take to heart the words of the poet Whittier:

> The substance of the life to be,
> We weave with materials all our own;
> And in the field of destiny,
> We reap as we have sown!

Rabbi Jesse J. Finkle

* * *

Keep Your Roof in Good Repair

The story is told about a certain dictator who one day ordered that the house of worship in one of the villages be taken over and used as a place of storage for army provisions. When this order reached the people, they became quite disturbed. They knew that the roof of their house of worship had been leaking for a number of months, and that if the military provisions were to be stored there, they would surely become spoiled. So they got to work immediately and repaired the roof. However, the order was changed and the house of worship was not to be taken over to be used as a storehouse.

This story reminds us of those among us who neglect our inner spiritual "house of faith," our religion. We pay little attention to the "leaks in the roof," until some outside force, some disturbing calamity, comes upon us, and we are made to realize how inadequate our "house of religious faith" is. It is then that we hasten to make the necessary "repairs."

Although it often happens that the "orders" are changed and approaching calamities often fail to come upon us, our "house of religious faith" must be kept in good repair by daily worship, Bible study, and the performance of good deeds. In this way, God's presence may become more manifest in our lives and we will come to feel more keenly His comforting and uplifting strength and guidance. Let us remember these words of a modern poet:

> Any religion, whatever it is, is only a rusty fetter.
> Your religion, mine or his, must make us better!

Rabbi Jesse J. Finkle

*   *   *

You Have to Be One to Give One

Have you seen any shooting stars recently? Most people think that shooting stars are simply meteorites burning up as they enter the earth's atmosphere. But I know that this is not always true. You may not believe this story, but last Wednesday night, long after my family went to sleep, I became a shooting star, flying across the heavens. But perhaps I should start from the beginning.

Wednesday was like any first day of Sukkot. Mrs. Gluckman and I brought up from the basement the large wooden frame for our Sukkah, and we set it up in the dining room. It hangs from the ceiling, like another roof, and, as is required by Jewish law, we can look up through it and see the stars. Our son Jonathan helped us decorate the Sukkah with corn stalks, fruits, and even some gourds. When we were finished it looked beautiful, as a Sukkah should. Sukkot is the Jewish Thanksgiving, so all the decorations in our Sukkah reminded us of the wonderful things God's earth provides to keep us alive. We even ate some bread and honey to symbolize our hope that the coming year would be sweet for us and for all people.

After we finished Kiddush a thought popped into my head. We should have our own lulav and ethrog to make the holiday complete.

After everyone had gone to sleep I went downstairs. I was sitting alone near the Sukkah when again the thought came to me that we should have our own lulav and ethrog. I couldn't get the idea out of my mind. It stuck there like a voice that wasn't even my own. Soon, I couldn't stand it anymore and I began to wish the voice would go away. Instead it became louder. Finally, it said, "Rabbi, you should have a lulav and an ethrog. Go out and get them. Beg for them."

And suddenly, I was dressed like a beggar, in old, worn clothes. I was still myself, but I felt different. I was cold, tired, and hungry. Then another miraculous thing happened. The ceiling of our Sukkah opened up and the clouds rolled away and the stars became visible. It was raining, but not on me. It was dark, but I could see. In fact, I could feel myself being lifted up out of my chair and being hurtled through the sky. I was a shooting star headed toward some distant place to beg for a lulav and an ethrog. Cities, towns, and time flashed by, and soon I found myself in a little village in a faraway land. Palm trees were growing all around, and I sought a palm leaf for my lulav. But I couldn't find one short enough to reach and I was too tired and weak to climb a tree, so I realized I would have to ask for one.

I soon found myself standing at the door of a beautiful home. Someone rich and powerful lives here, I imagined. I will ask him for a palm branch.

It was cold as I knocked on the door. No one answered, even though many lights were on. I knocked again and the door flew open, but no one was there. I called out, "Is anybody here?" Again and again I called, but no one answered. After waiting for what seemed like an eternity, a man, obviously someone of breeding and fortune, came into the living room. As he approached me I could see he was shivering from the cold and very angry.

"What do you want, beggar?" he said. "I came to ask you for a palm branch for my lulav," I replied. He looked at me with hostile eyes and said: "Wait here." I waited a long time but he did not return. Finally I decided to look for him. I searched the house but he was gone. I looked in the backyard and there I found him, shivering in the dark cold Sukkah, hiding from me. "Why are you hiding from me?" I asked. "Because I don't want to give you anything," he said, "but as long as you have found me, here is the palm branch you asked for." The palm branch for the lulav is supposed to be tall and straight and proud looking. What he handed me was broken and wilted from the cold. It looked very sad. And so did he. His pride was gone.

As I turned to go, clutching the palm leaf in my hand, my miracle of flight repeated itself. I was a shooting star again on my way to another spot on earth to complete my lulav set. When I came down it was in a big city. Fluorescent lights flashed on and off, advertising stores and markets. People were still on the streets and I was standing before a home that was all aglow with the lights of a party. I thought they might be celebrating Sukkot, so I knocked on the door. A lady and her husband came to answer, and they were shocked to see me. "Who are you?" they asked. "I have come to ask if you could give me an ethrog," I replied. They both stared in wonder. "Come in, we are having a little celebration for our anniversary," they said, "and we didn't know today is a holiday." "In fact," said the man, "I haven't even

233

heard or thought of Sukkot since I was a little boy. Go up in the attic and there among some old books I think you will find an ethrog my father once gave me." I climbed the stairs and searched among some old books. There were books of Jewish stories and history, books of Talmud and Torah. All of them were dirty and unused. Between the pages of an ancient Bible I found pressed an old, shriveled ethrog. It had no sweet odor left and instead of being a beautiful yellow, it was dark brown. It was as worthless as a rotten tomato. But I took it anyway.

As I walked through the living room, all the people looked at me. I must have been a strange sight, with my broken palm and shriveled ethrog. I am sure they were as mystified as I was as to what this was all about.

Suddenly I was gone, dashing through the air like a shooting star, headed for another land and another city. This time I found myself in a place where the ambassadors of many nations meet to solve their problems together. Here were people dressed in clothes like ours and in robes and turbans. Men of high station of every race and nation were there, yellow, black, white, and brown people. All were supposed to be working for peace. But when they saw me they were appalled. "Get this fool out!" they cried, angrily. "Guards! Guards! Get him out. We want no beggars in here!" "Wait," I said, "I don't mean to disturb you. I have merely come to ask for a piece of willow, that humble-looking tree, for my lulav" "Get out!" they all howled. "We are not concerned with small matters, only things of great importance concern us. We decide where to fight and

234

where to retreat, which nations shall live and which shall die. Ours are the problems of all mankind. We have no time for you." Almost in tears I said, "But all I need is a willow bough. Can't you help me?"

The leader of the group then spoke, "Send him into the courtyard. We have no humble willows here. But at least he can pick a palm leaf to replace that broken one in his hand."

A guard grabbed me by the collar to lead me to the courtyard. But as we reached the door a miracle happened. The whole wall disappeared and there in the courtyard were no palms at all, just dozens of lovely willow trees. As they watched in amazement I picked a piece of willow and added it to my collection. I then walked to the leader's chair and said: "You have seen a miracle here tonight. You have been arrogant, and the humble willow has taught you a lesson. Now you shall see another miracle." And in the twinkling of an eye all the papers on his desk and on the desks of all the ambassadors turned into beautiful little myrtle plants. "Don't forget," I said, "the decisions you make here are to help all the people of the world. You have to be humble like the willow before you can truly make the life of the world's millions any safer and more prosperous. The symbol for the ordinary man is the myrtle on your desk."

With that I picked a piece of myrtle from his desk and disappeared across the sky in a streak of light as bright as a shooting star, carrying the completed lulav in my hand and the wrinkled ethrog in my pocket.

When I came to my senses again I was sitting before

the Sukkah in my dining room. The room was dark, so I turned on the light. There before me, standing under the Sukkah, were not the broken palm and the shriveled ethrog, but a straight and beautiful palm with lovely willow and myrtle branches and a beautiful yellow, scented ethrog.

I wondered about the meaning of what had happened. I then realized that the lesson was you have to *be* what you give away, that you are what you give to others. The man who gave me the palm leaf, though he was rich and powerful, could never give me the dignified, straight palm. All he could give was a withered one. So if we want to teach charity, great-heartedness, and dignity to one another, we have to be that way ourselves.

The people at the party could never have given me the bright yellow, scented ethrog because it is a symbol of pious and educated Jews. They didn't even know it was Sukkot. And their books of Jewish knowledge were covered with dust. You have to be educated and observant to teach others.

And the ambassadors in the Council of Nations were so rude and thoughtless of the lives of their people that their gift to me could only be the humble willow, a lesson that they should stop being arrogant and self-centered and start being considerate of others.

We all have these lessons to learn: To be straight, upright, and charitable, like the palm; humble like the willow, and pious and educated like the ethrog. And, above all, we must be considerate of the myrtle, the common people, because that's what we all are.

You may be skeptical of my story. You don't think

it's true. "How could the Rabbi become a shooting star?" you ask. But whether or not the story is true the moral surely is.

And one last thing: You know I said I put the shriveled brown ethrog the man and wife gave me in my pocket for the journey home. Well, believe it or not, I found it yesterday in the same pocket. I still have it. Here it is, living proof that my tale is true.

Rabbi Donald N. Gluckman

* * *

A Compass

I have in my hand a compass.

A compass is an instrument containing a magnetic needle which is mounted on a pivot so that it can turn freely. The needle always points in the direction of the magnetic north or south poles.

We humans do not have the capacity to home in on a geographical place. Yet we see that animals do. A dog has the instinctive ability to come home from another part of town. The homing pigeon can be transported in a dark box many miles. No sooner is it released in a new place, then it will take off in the right direction and unerringly find its way home. This is true also of swallows, geese, and ducks. Zoologists are baffled by this wonder of nature.

Is it possible that the Creator endowed a creature as little as a bird with an internal compass, while He left man without a sense of direction and without guidance to find his way?

The truth of the matter is that the Creator has provided us with the greatest and best guide in the world, namely the Torah. Torah means "guidance." It is our true guide in life. Without it mankind would still be enslaved to primitive notions of the world, full of superstitions and fears. It is the Torah which has guided us out of the mire of barbarism to democratic living. The Torah is our perfect compass.

Some people mistakenly think that Judaism has no set creed or dogmas. But this is not so. Our ancestors, the great prophets of Israel, brought to mankind a unique concept of God. Not only is He the God who created the world and is the architect of the cosmic order which scientists can measure and study, He is also our Heavenly Father. This is why prayers are addressed to Our Heavenly Father, He who is concerned with man's welfare and who at one point in our history revealed to us a Divine way of life.

Have you ever set a radio alarm to wake you to the sound of the morning news? I did once last week, and I didn't know whether I was listening to the news or having a nightmare. The local news was of car accidents, robbery in broad daylight, or prison escapes, of graft and dishonesty among public officials. The world news was as frightening, only on a larger scale: the East against the West, Russia against China, China against America, the Arabs against Israel.

238

What is the cause of all this?

Today we need to reflect on who we are, what we are, and what is to be our place in the world.

God gave His code to all of mankind, yet mankind often ignores the beautiful system of morality and ethics devised by God.

There is only one hope. That in each of us there is a "small voice," an inner voice, a conscience. Before radar, before sonar, before the compass, the Eternal provided each descendant of Adam with a built-in navigational direction finder.

A pain in my tooth is a warning of mercy. It tells me that I need a dentist. A pain in my leg tells me that I need a physician. My tooth and other parts of my body are too important to trifle with, so I do something to prevent illness and I listen to the symptoms which are warning signals.

Your conscience is saying something each day. It tells you not to trifle with your soul, with the pure soul that God gave you at birth. Let us be guided by the two aids that our Almighty Father has given us to enoble our lives. His Torah contains the answer to all of world problems. It has in it the solutions to race riots, crime, and wars. But if not applied, if left in the ark, God's message goes undelivered. Only when man listens to the "small voice within" will he be able to benefit and respond to the voice of God which emanated from Mount Sinai.

God gave us a compass by which to direct our steps. Let us use it and not get lost.

Rabbi Irving Rubin

239

Change

Do you think that prayer can change things?
This question is often asked.

The answer is probably that prayer can not change things, but that it can change us enough so that we will go out and change things.

For, one of the marvels of life is our ability to change.

Some do not believe we are capable of altering our lives.

We often hear people say: ''You know how human nature is. And as long as human nature is the way it is, there will always be war and troubles in the world.''

Or we ourselves are prone to say sometimes, when we are chided for some fault or when we think about it: ''Well, that's the way I am,'' or ''That's the way I'm made.''

The notion that we are made in such a way and that therefore we are unable to improve disregards the power we often display to become a bit different, to grow out of our shortcomings, to rise to a higher level of conduct.

One of the greatest miracles worked by God is the capacity He has given us to grow, to grow out of our faults, if only we try hard enough. True, it can't be done instantaneously. But if we work at it we can become better, more considerate, more restrained, more skillful.

And prayer is the beginning of the process. When we pray and acknowledge our indebtedness to God and seek to attune our will to His, we begin the slow, up-

240

ward march to liberation from our follies, our faults, and our shortcomings.

So let us pray often and then do something about our prayers so that we will fulfil the urgings within us implanted by Almighty God.

Rabbi Samuel M. Silver

* * *

To Be Grateful is To Be Great

In the autumn in homes and synagogues throughout the world the holiday of Sukkos is observed.

Sukkos is a Hebrew word which means tabernacles or tents.

When the holiday is celebrated the worshipper remembers that for forty years the Israelites wandered in the desert in their freedom march from Egypt to Old Canaan.

For forty years the pilgrims lived in tents, or sukkos, and during all that time they were granted the protection of the God Whom they worshipped.

In remembrance of that hegira, the holiday of Sukkos was instituted. As we think of the frail abodes in which the wanderers dwelt we feel an upsurge of gratitude to God for His aid.

Indeed, the Jewish holiday of Sukkos is the model after which the Pilgrims patterned our American Thanksgiving Day.

The pilgrims looked upon themselves as the succes-

241

sors of the ancient Israelites. They were oppressed by despotism, and so were the Pilgrims. They crossed a trackless area in quest of the Promised Land, and so did the Pilgrims. They proclaimed a holiday of appreciation to God, and so did the Pilgrims in this blessed land which they had reached after their travels and their travails.

The theme of the holiday of Sukkos is gratitude. There is nothing Jewish about gratitude. It is universal. It applies to all men. To be grateful is to be great. May we display our appreciation for what we have received from ancient benefactors and from the inspiring people of our own time. And may we so act that other people will feel thankful towards us.

Rabbi Samuel M. Silver

Terrible?

"It's a terrible day today. It's raining."

I heard some one characterize the weather in that way not so long ago.

It was raining . . . so the day was terrible.

Ah, how fragmentary is our vision and how often our outlook is selfish.

Does rain make a day terrible?

Without that rain would the earth be nourished? If the earth were not bathed ever so often, where would our food come from? The next time it rains forget yourself.

Imagine yourself to be a farmer who looks with anxiety on every day which means the parching of his soil. His soil? Our soil. God's soil, the repository of the food we

242

eat, the source of our energy and our health.

Practice unselfishness. The next time it rains forget your own immediate discomfiture and see that phenomenon of nature in its grander scope. Or echo the words of the poet William Stidger, who once sang:

> I saw God wash the world last night
> With His sweet showers on high,
> And then when morning came
> I saw Him hang it out to dry.
>
> He washed each tiny blade of grass
> And every trembling tree,
> He flung His showers against the hill,
> And swept the billowing sea.
>
> The white rose is a cleaner white,
> The red rose is more red,
> Since God washed every fragrant face,
> And put them all to bed.
>
> There's not a bird, there's not a bee that wings along
>   the way
> But is a cleaner bird and bee than it was yesterday.
> I saw God wash the world last night, Ah, would He had
>   washed me
> As clean of all my dust and dirt, As that old white birch
>   tree.''

What a wonderful day it is when we are favored with the blessing of rain. May we always appreciate the glories of nature, reflecting the wisdom of Almighty God.

Rabbi Samuel M. Silver

243